Beauma

YALE UNIVERSITY PRESS   NEW HAVEN & LONDON

rchais

in

Seville

An Intermezzo

Hugh Thomas

Copyright © 2006 by Hugh Thomas.
All rights reserved. This book may not be reproduced, in whole or in part,
including illustrations, in any form (beyond that copying permitted by
Sections 107 and 108 of the U.S. Copyright Law and except by reviewers
for the public press), without written permission from the publishers.

Designed by Mary Valencia.
Set in Adobe Caslon by Duke & Company, Devon, Pennsylvania.
Printed in the United States of America.

Library of Congress Cataloging-in-Publication Data

Thomas, Hugh, 1931–
Beaumarchais in Seville : an intermezzo / Hugh Thomas.
p.   cm.
Includes bibliographical references and index.
ISBN-13: 978-0-300-12103-2 (cloth : alk. paper)
ISBN-10: 0-300-12103-2 (cloth : alk. paper)
1. Beaumarchais, Pierre Augustin Caron de, 1732–1799—Travel—Spain—Madrid.
2. Dramatists, French—18th century—Biography. I. Title.
PQ1956.T45 2006
842′.5—dc22
[B]   2006013533

A catalogue record for this book is available from the British Library.

The paper in this book meets the guidelines for permanence and durability
of the Committee on Production Guidelines for Book Longevity
of the Council on Library Resources.

10 9 8 7 6 5 4 3 2 1

My inexhaustible good humour never left me for a moment.

—Beaumarchais to his father about his stay in Madrid,
January 28, 1765

Contents

Contents

Note on Currencies

12.6 louis = 1 livre

3 livres = 1 écu

Preface

B ut Beaumarchais was never in Seville! No; and nor was Mozart, nor Rossini. Nor, for that matter, did Bizet, Verdi, or Beethoven, go there, though they all placed famous works in that city or in its surroundings. But all the same these men have made Seville what it is, or at least what it is thought to be outside Spain, and their creations, such as (in the case of Beaumarchais) Figaro and the Count of Almaviva, Rosina, and Susanna, have become the most internationally famous of Sevillanos. They are among the best known and most loved of all artistic creations.

In this book I shall consider how it was that Beaumarchais met the inspiration for those and other characters when he was in Madrid or nearby—in Aranjuez, La Granja, or the Escorial—during his stay in Castile in 1764 and 1765.

Of course, all great writers invent their characters. The Baron de Charlus is not an exact replica of Robert de Montesquiou, nor has Mr. Pickwick a clear connection with anyone. All the same, Beaumarchais found in Spain a way of living in which he could permit his fascinating creations to live, talk, sing, dance, flirt, argue—and flourish.

Why, it will be asked, did he set his two most successful plays in Seville when he could have no idea what that magical city was really like? Presumably because it was the capital of Spain's vast empire in the Americas, where treasure fleets had been bringing gold and silver, pearls and emeralds, for more than two hundred years. Perhaps also because it seemed to be where the enchanting dances of Spain originated. Whatever the reason, Beaumarchais set Seville on its new, modern, romantic course. A fortress near Seville (Beethoven)? A village between Seville and Córdoba (Verdi)? The immortal tobacco factory (Merimée and Bizet)? Inventiveness continued till Seville built her own opera house in 1992! Sitting now as I am in a magnificent patio in a restored palace of the seventeenth century, by a fountain of a complex design surrounded by palms and red lilies, my reflection is "What a pity Beaumarchais never came here!"

I would like to thank Monsieur Hubert Faure for his hospitality in Normandy, where I completed the book.

Dramatis Personae

FRENCH CHARACTERS

LOUIS XV, King of France

MADAME DE POMPADOUR, his mistress

His Daughters

ADÉLAÏDE

LOUISE-ELIZABETH, married to the Duke of Parma and mother
of Queen María Luisa, who married the Prince of Asturias,
later King Charles IV

VICTOIRE ("MADAME VICTOIRE")

SOPHIE

Dramatis Personae

The Caron Family

ANDRÉ-CHARLES CARON, watchmaker of Paris

His Children

JEANNE-MARGUERITE ("TONTON"), pursued by, and eventually
married to, JEAN-BAPTISTE JANOT DE MORON, a courtier

MADELEINE-FRANÇOISE CARON ("FANCHON"), married to
JEAN-ANTOINE LÉPINE, watchmaker

MARIE-JOSÈPHE CARON, married to Louis Guilbert

MARIE-LOUISE CARON ("LISETTE")

MARIE-JULIE CARON ("BÉCASSE")

PIERRE-AUGUSTIN CARON, later known as CARON DE
BEAUMARCHAIS

Other French Characters

MADELEINE-CATHERINE AUBERTIN, widow of Pierre-Augustin
Franquet, and Beaumarchais's first wife

JEAN-ANDRÉ LEPAUTE, master watchmaker

COMTE DE SAINT-FLORENTIN, minister to the king

THEODORE TRONCHIN, doctor from Geneva

DUC DE CHOISEUL, minister for foreign affairs

JOSEPH PÂRIS-DUVERNEY, financier

DUC DE LA VALLIÈRE, bibliophile, captain-general of the *chasses
au bailliage*

PRÉVILLE, actor and old friend of the Carons

PAULINE LE BRETON, possible fiancée of Beaumarchais in 1763,
heiress to a property in Saint-Domingue (now in Haiti)

Dramatis Personae

JEAN DURAND, French businessman in Madrid

MARQUIS D'AUBARÈDE, fellow traveller with Beaumarchais to Spain

PÉRIER, businessman hired by Caron to protect Beaumarchais

PIERRE-PAUL OSSUN, MARQUIS and BARON DE HELCHES ET SAINT-LUC, French ambassador in Spain

CHARACTERS IN SPAIN

CHARLES III, king of Spain, first cousin to Louis XV

JOSÉ CLAVIJO Y FAJARDO, enlightened journalist of Madrid, supposed fiancé of Lisette Caron

RICHARD WALL, Irish general in the service of Spain, ex-minister

JERÓNIMO GRIMALDI, Genoese, who came with Charles III from Naples, minister of foreign affairs in Spain

LEOPOLDO DE GREGORIO, MARQUÉS DE SQUILLACE, minister of finance and war in Spain (Spanish usage employed)

JULIÁN DE ARRIAGA, minister of marine in Spain

AMERIGO PINI, Italian valet to King Charles III

COLONEL DE ROBIOU, military commandant of Madrid

ANTONIO DE PORTUGUÉS, civil servant and friend of Clavijo

MIGUEL DE URIARTE, Basque businessman established in Cádiz

RAMÓN DE LA CRUZ, author of *"sainetes"*

MARÍA LADVENANT, actress of Madrid

DEBTORS OF CARON IN MADRID

DUQUESA DE BOURNONVILLE

Dramatis Personae

ANTONIO PATIÑO, MARQUÉS DE CASTELAR

MIGUEL FERRER, Catalan businessman

CONDESA-DUQUESA DE BENAVENTE

CONDESA DE UCEDA

FRIENDS OF BEAUMARCHAIS IN SPAIN

CONDESA DE FUENCLARA, old friend of Caron, widow of a viceroy in New Spain

DUQUE DE SAN BLAS, gambling friend of Beaumarchais in Madrid

CHEVALIER DE GUZMÁN, the same

MARQUÉS DE CARRASOLA, the same

FRANCISCO-CARLOS, MARQUÉS DE CROIX, governor-general of Galicia

FERNANDE, MARQUESA DE CROIX, his wife

MONSEIGNEUR DE JARENTE, bishop of Orléans, her uncle

MONSEIGNEUR ACQUAVIVA, papal vice legate at Avignon, her one-time lover, subsequently CARDINAL

WILLIAM HENRY ZUYLESTEIN, LORD ROCHFORD, British ambassador to Madrid

PETER COUNT OF BUTURLIN, Russian ambassador to Madrid

MARIA ROMANOVNA, his wife

The POSTMASTER OF AUDÍCANA (VITORIA) and his daughter-in-law

NOTE: I have Anglicised the titles of address for Beaumarchais's character the COUNT OF ALMAVIVA and for the COUNT OF BITURLIN. All other titles are rendered according to contemporary local usage.

ONE

A Golden Age

In 1764 peace reigned in all four continents: Europe, Asia, America, and Africa. Australia had not been discovered. The Tsarina Catherine was in correspondence with Voltaire, whose *Dictionnaire philosophique* was published that year. The king of France, with his black eyes, was the best-looking monarch to be seen on a throne for many years. The English colonies in North America calmly contemplated an imperial future, and George Washington thought himself a loyal British officer. Italians flocked to the light-hearted plays of Goldoni, and in Spain foreigners were entranced by the wild dance known as the fandango. England had a prime minister nicknamed "The Gentle Shepherd." Napoleon had not been born. Socialism did not exist, not even as a word. Nationalism had not been invented: the proof of which was that the two most important ministers at the Spanish Court were Italians. The ceiling of the royal palace in Madrid was being decorated by the Venetian Giambattista Tiepolo with a fresco depicting Spain's worldwide supremacy: Jupiter, presiding over the universe, commands Mercury, bearing a crown, and Apollo, carrying a sceptre, bestows authority to the country over her dominions throughout the world.

In Paris, it was said, the age of passion was giving way to that of wit. Certainly, the solemn preachers of the early eighteenth century had given way to light entertainers, such as Massillon, whose later work was so entertaining that Voltaire had him read aloud when he dined alone. The use of torture had diminished throughout Europe, even in Russia. The Spanish Inquisition had modified its rigorous rules. At that time the Industrial Revolution had not begun, even in England, though a few iron wheels already defaced her countryside. But most towns remained beautiful: even their suburbs.

The watchmakers of Paris were busier than ever, conscious that they had devised "a technological breakthrough," which would outlive every other contemporary invention: the watch. In particular, the workshop of André-Charles Caron was busy, since that master's son, who is known to history as Beaumarchais, had devised a new way of ensuring accuracy of those wonderful devices.

Beaumarchais had been born Pierre-Augustin Caron in 1732. He had entered the world without the agreeably particuled "de Beaumarchais" for which he became later known. An apprentice watchmaker seemed at that time to have the world at his feet, since watches were in those days beginning to be important with everyone who counted in society. For this was when it was first possible for those who could afford it to carry these "timepieces" on their persons. A true revolution! In the past, church bells had tolled the hours. If one were out of earshot of a church clock, one still thought in Roman terms, of the "first hour" or of "an hour before sunset." Now punctuality was possible. The new age was proclaimed by King Louis XIV standing in Versailles with a stopwatch in his hand. A minister arrived on the stroke of ten in the morning. The king said, "Ah, monsieur, you almost made me wait."

Till that time, appointments had all been approximate in nature. But once the pocket watch made its appearance, with an hour hand, a minute hand, and, sometimes—what luxury—a special dial with a second hand, all would change. The watchmakers of Paris were the aristocrats of this new world. Were they not as important to France as the sugar makers of Mauritius and Martinique who could become barons merely because they sweetened the Parisians' cups of chocolate?

Beaumarchais's father, Caron, was an inventor as well as a watchmaker. In 1729 he made a "new machine enabling boats to sail upstream on rivers." He was denounced thereby for stealing the patent of a rival, François Tavernier de Boullonge, but he easily survived the accusation. He was a well-read man, and in particular he loved the novels of Samuel Richardson, *Pamela, Clarissa,* and *Sir Charles Grandison:* like Pushkin's Tatiana in *Eugene Onegin,* he had "on Richardson gone raving mad." Beaumarchais thought his father "far the most precious treasure which I possess." In return, the father paid his son the supreme compliment (for him) of comparing him with the noble figure of Sir Charles Grandison, the hero of Richardson's most recent novel.

The family of Caron came originally from Lizy-sur-Ourq, near Meaux, about twenty miles east of Paris. They then moved to the rue Saint-André-des-Arts, in the sixth arrondissement, then as now a street lined by fine palaces, such as that which had once belonged to Jeanne, the wife of King Philippe le Bel. Voltaire had been born in one of them a few years before. The Carons lived afterwards in "the great street of Saint-Denis," which was then the longest, richest, and most beautiful in Paris. Their house and workshop was at what is now no. 30, on the angle of the rue de la Ferronerie. The latter street, too, had been important in the history of France, for in front of no. 11, King Henry IV had been murdered in 1610 by the fanatical Catholic Ravaillac, putting an end to that monarch's grand dream of a new Europe under French inspiration. Much later, Jeanne Bécu had been an errand girl in a clothes shop nearby named Labille, long before she became famous as the Comtesse du Barry, Louis XV's last mistress. In another clothes shop in the same street, a model of the painter Boucher, Mademoiselle Morphise or Morfil (actually Murphy to begin with), was to embark on her interesting life, in which she too caught the attention of the king, in the scandalous brothel le Parc aux Cerfs.

Beaumarchais—for so I shall call him even though he was not so named for a time—was born in the rue Saint-Denis. He had a delightful childhood since he was the only surviving boy among five girls. His sisters called him "Brother Charming" or "Pierrot," and they all danced together, played music, recited, and wrote both music and verses. Perhaps the boy Beaumarchais was a Cherubino among all his sisters—though, as his best biographer, the late Maurice Lever put it, "a cherubino with teeth." The lively street outside was full of games, musicians, cries, and performers too. Life in such roadways with horses and coaches was far more gay than it is today with motor vehicles exercising their despotic menaces. There the child must have learned a lot.

The family was broken up by an unusual proposal. One of the richest agents of Caron, in Spain, passed through Paris and made the curious suggestion, "Give me two of your girls and I will take them to Madrid. They can establish themselves with me, an elderly bachelor with no family. They will make my old age happy, and I shall leave them the most valuable shop in Spain." Marie-Joséphe Caron jumped at the idea as a way of escaping from her drunken, unfaithful, and unsuccessful husband; and she and her youngest sister Lisette (Marie-Louise), then aged seventeen, went to live in Madrid in 1748.

To assist this unusual arrangement, Caron agreed to send more watches and clocks to sell to the Spanish upper class. There were then in the Spanish capital a substantial number of French bankers, merchants, and manufacturers, not to speak of Paris-born shopkeepers, cabinet makers, and pastry cooks. So Beaumarchais's sisters would be far from lonely foreigners in a distant city.

But after two years, the rich old man died, as if for all the world the Caron sisters were living in a bad fairy story: he left the girls nothing but the shop, which they had to maintain alone. But they succeeded in this, "thanks to their commercial skills, to their charm of manner, and to a crowd of friends keen to increase their credit and their standing." The sisters were soon famous in Madrid as "las Caronas."

The young Beaumarchais himself meantime was employed as an apprentice to his father. Watchmakers then had an obligation to sit in full view of passers-by. This was an order imposed by the jewellers' association to prevent the practitioner using anything but precious metals. So Beaumarchais would do his work in the window of his father's shop in the rue Saint-Denis.

Watches were then made in many extraordinary shapes: as shells, olives, fleurs-de-lys, pears, even tulips. There was a cult of such things among the fashionable. Smart people often had one gold watch and one silver one.

A weakness of the timepieces of those days was that they all went too fast. That was because the wheels of the mechanism were moved by a spring which acted without interruption, inaccurately accelerating the watch. A brake was necessary to prevent the wheels from turning too quickly without stopping them altogether. This appliance was known as the "échappement"—a word whose literal translation is "escapement." A big technological step forward had been taken with the invention of the spiral balance spring in 1675. But that was not enough.

The young Beaumarchais began to think about this matter

in 1751, when he was nineteen. He worked hard and made use of the work of two Scotsmen, Thomas Tompion and his gifted pupil George Graham, who had been the masters in the field for years. Though both were dead and buried (in Westminster Abbey, no less), Graham had made a cylinder escapement in a modern form and sent it to Paris for the attention of Julien le Roy, at that time the greatest horologist of France. Eventually, inspired by this, Beaumarchais, still only twenty-one, constructed a lever which did what was wanted and put it in a watch. He made this interesting invention in July 1753.

He kept his friends and the friends of his father well informed, among them a clockmaker of the court, Jean-André Lepaute, who had observed his activities from the street. Lepaute, then aged forty-five, had made the first horizontal clock for the Palais du Luxembourg, and had also created clocks for the Tuileries, the Palais Royal, and the Jardin des Plantes. Indeed, most of the imposing new timepieces of Paris had been made by him. Lepaute was successful and powerful. On July 23, 1753, he looked very carefully at the new escapement shown to him with such understandable pride by the young Beaumarchais; that September, Beaumarchais was beside himself with rage to read, in the leading intellectual journal, *Le Mercure de France,* that Lepaute was calling himself the author of this new development. Beaumarchais wrote to protest in a letter published in that journal on November 15. Lepaute replied in January 1754, accompanying his defence with a certificate signed by three Jesuits who agreed that he had talked to them of an invention of this nature the previous May.

The Royal Academy of Sciences was summoned by the Comte de Saint-Florentin, minister "de la maison du roi," to pronounce on the matter. That nobleman had been regent of France when in 1744 the king had gone to lead the army in Flanders. He was intolerant: it was said of him that, by 1774, there had been no new opinion and no new religious or political view during the previous half-century for which he had not exiled the author. But all the same, Beaumarchais sent another statement of fifteen pages to the Royal Academy, insisting that the invention was his. On February 24, 1754, the Academy gave the verdict: "Monsieur Caron must be regarded as the real author of the new lever for watches."

This triumph, a victory over the established authority in his family profession, made Beaumarchais's career. He devised a pocket watch ("montre à gousset") for the king; another miniaturised version of it, in the form of a ring, for Madame de Pompadour, the king's powerful mistress, was wound by a lever projecting from the case under the dial. He made, too, a little pendular clock for Madame Victoire (the king's daughter, Louise-Thérèse Victoire). Within a few months, the brilliant young Beaumarchais became known to all the royal family. He signed himself "Caron fils Horloger du Roi." He was successful, too, in other ways: "From the moment that Beaumarchais arrived in Versailles," wrote his friend Gudin de la Brenellerie, "all the women were struck by his height, his elegant figure, the regularity of his features, his assured look, his lively mien, the dominating air which he seemed to have and which seemed to elevate everything and everyone surrounding him." But the more women loved him, the more suspicions he aroused among men.

He then took a considered decision to devote the next ten years of his life to making his fortune. He wrote to his father in 1754, "I shall soon be twenty-three. I wish absolutely that the years which will pass till before I am forty will, after heavy work, bring me to the sweet tranquillity which I believe is only truly agreeable when one sees it as the compensation for the struggles of youth. . . . I work, I write, I discuss, I dictate, I exhibit, I fight: such is my life."

Voltaire, it may be said, had taken the same hard decision as Beaumarchais in respect of his finances thirty years before: "I saw so many poor and despised men of letters," he wrote, "that I decided . . . not to add to their number. . . . There is always one way or another by which a private individual can profit without incurring any obligation to anyone; and nothing is so agreeable as to make one's fortune." In 1755 Beaumarchais had himself painted by the fashionable Jean-Marc Nattier, painter to the royal family. It was a remarkable portrait for a watchmaker to commission. As usual, the painter arranged for the sitter to emerge with rich rosy cheeks.

From the end of 1755 to the end of 1756, Beaumarchais had another interest which was not far removed from his quest for advancement. He began to be friendly with Madeleine-Catherine Aubertin, the wife of Pierre-Augustin Franquet, an elderly, perhaps decrepit, official with a desirable sinecure at Versailles, currently "contrôleur-clerc d'office de la maison du roi." Such long titles usually suggested well-paid inactivity. He was fifteen years older than his wife, and she was ten years older than Beaumarchais. She met Beaumarchais in Versailles and then went to the rue Saint-Denis to have a watch mended by him: a pretext. On the brink of senility, Franquet died early in January 1756. In November of that year, Beaumarchais succeeded him as "contrôleur-clerc." That enabled him to precede, sword at his side, the arrival of the large legs of lamb or ribs of beef into the royal dining room.

Then, only ten months after her widowhood, Beaumarchais married Madeleine-Catherine at Saint-Nicolas des Champs, in the Temple quarter, defying the church's rules that a widow or widower should wait a year after the death of the spouse. Beaumarchais went to live in the rue de Braque (between the rues des Archives and du Temple) with his new wife and his mother-in-law, Catherine Aubertin. Police reports cited by Maurice Lever show that Beaumarchais often frequented well-known ladies of easy virtue in those days. It is not evident that his marriage interrupted those visits.

The next year, because of his wife, Beaumarchais was able to buy the useful-sounding but meaningless title of secretary of the king. That, in turn, by a curious dispensation, enabled to him to call himself by the surname of Beaumarchais. For old Franquet had bought at Vert-le-Grand, now Valgrand (Essonne), in the parish of Arpajon, a country house known by the name of its preceding owner, Beaumarchais or Beaumarchet. Franquet's successor called himself that for the first time in September 1757, first as "Caron de Beaumarchais," later just "de Beaumarchais." Beginning in December 1759 this use of the grand name was officially allowed.

Almost immediately, Beaumarchais's new wife fell ill of a "malign fever." He called in the best doctor whom he knew, Theodore Tronchin, of a famous family of Geneva, a friend of Voltaire's and of the banking family the Neckers, as he had been once of the English statesman Bolingbroke. Tronchin was a good doctor if an unprincipled man, a pupil of the pioneer of inoculation, Boerhaave, but he could not save Beaumarchais's wife. She died soon after. Some of her husband's kind friends accused him of poisoning her.

Beaumarchais left the house of his mother-in-law and went to live in 17 Basse-du-Rempart, in a fashionable new district in Paris near the Madeleine.

These events in his personal life did not seem to slow Beaumarchais's steady rise in society. On the contrary. He continued to call himself de Beaumarchais. It sounded much more chic than Caron. In 1759 he became music teacher to the four princesses of France—the quick-walking, shy Sophie; the charming Victoire, the king's favourite daughter; Adélaïde, masculine and brusque, called "la Ridicule" by her mother; and Louise-Élizabeth, "Madame Dernière," who soon married the Duke of Parma. These princesses were half Polish (their mother had been Maria Lesczczyńska), and their father, whom they loved, referred to them by most unbecoming nicknames.

As his childhood had shown, Beaumarchais had an ear for music, and he was almost as good a singer and harpist as he had been a watchmaker. The harp in particular attracted his attention and that of his princesses. That instrument in its modern form was new, having been introduced into Paris in 1749 in the orchestra of a rich tax farmer Le Riche de La Pouplinière, a patron of the arts. It seems to have first been brought to Versailles by a Bavarian violin maker, Christian Höchbrücker. The artist Greuze depicted another senior official, the chief of protocol, Ange La Live de Jully, playing one in a picture exhibited in 1759 in the grand salon of painting.

Beaumarchais was often asked to buy instruments for the princesses. Thus in January 1764 he found a tambourine for Madame Victoire, as well as a flute. He now gave his form of address as "Monsieur de Beaumarchais, contrôleur de la maison du roi au bureau Dauphin à Versailles." He organised little concerts every week at the court, himself playing, say, the sonatas of the popular Italian Carlo Chiabrano (Chabran) or singing the songs of Jean-Benjamin de Laborde, who subsequently was his close friend. He also wrote such one-act plays as "Jean-Bête à la foire" (Jean-Bête at the fair), "Les bottes de sept lieues" (The seven-league boots), and "Léandre, marchand d'agnus" (Leander the lamb merchant). One biographer of Beaumarchais, Pierre Larthomas, thought that "Figaro without doubt would not have been so remarkable had he not had as elder brothers Léandre and Jean-Bête." These characters were working-class impertinents who sang and danced their way out of trouble. Beaumarchais seems to have identified himself with them when he was not trying to be an aristocrat.

But he was not consumed by artistic considerations. In the

spring of 1760 he was invited to the château of Charles-Guillaume le Normant d'Étiolles, the complaisant husband of Madame de Pompadour ("cocu et content"—cuckold and content—as E. J. Arnould put it): the first performance of "Jean-Bête" had been given in Charles's honour. At this party, Beaumarchais met the remarkable financier Joseph Pâris-Duverney. He was then aged seventy-five and was one of four self-made brothers from Moirans in the Isère who had made fortunes providing arms and other supplies to the French army from the War of the Spanish Succession onwards. The brothers had risen partly thanks to the support of women: Agnès de Prie, the beautiful if doomed mistress of the Duc de Bourbon when he had been prime minister (and also of Voltaire; she died by her own hand soon after leaving the Court); Marie Anne, Duchesse de Châteauroux, who became King Louis XV's mistress in the 1740s; and, above all, Madame de Pompadour, who had the same status with the king in the 1750s. She called Pâris-Duverney her "dear fathead" and considered him her great confidant. He had also helped to make the fortune of Voltaire, whom he had met in 1725, and the author of *Candide* always spoke warmly of him: "I look on him as one of the best and most useful of citizens that France has ever had."

Admittedly, the journal *Correspondance littéraire* at Pâris-Duverney's death would write that he "saw the safety of France at the end of his rifle"; and he had encouraged French entry into the Seven Years' War, a catastrophe. Yet all the same he had built the military school at Saint-Cyr on the suggestion of Madame de

Pompadour, who had followed every detail of the work with attention, and he was now looking for new investments. A portrait of him in July 1757 by Van Loo, in a full-bottomed wig, suggests that at seventy-three he was in fine shape.

Pâris-Duverney, a widower without children—at least without legitimate children—was, like so many, fascinated by the young Beaumarchais and offered him "his heart, his support, and his credit." Beaumarchais became the son whom Pâris-Duverney had never had. They communicated in innumerable letters in a kind of code: they spoke of a great financial opportunity as if it were the chance of a new mistress, while a new commercial opening was spoken of as if it were a love affair. Whatever the exact truth of their relationship, Pâris-Duverney certainly thought, as Maurice Lever put it, that Beaumarchais had "audacity, a taste for risk, a spirit of enterprise, political intelligence, a gift with people, a strong sense of self-confidence, and, above all, an appetite for wealth which he does not even try and hide." It was true; and it might be a slogan for a graduate of a business school in modern times. So Pâris-Duverney made available to Beaumarchais 6,000 livres a year, an arrangement far from the liking of the financier's nephews, as would be shown to be the case after his death. Pâris-Duverney also lent him 55,000 francs so that he could become Chevet du roi. The new office meant that he had to sign a few letters to suppliants on the king's behalf, but it also gave him privileges, including the rank of nobility "of the first degree," transmissible to his heirs on condition of his having enjoyed the position at least twenty years.

Beaumarchais wanted to be a nobleman. But that was impossible if his father continued a mere watchmaker. Caron was as infatuated by his son as was Pâris-Duverney and would do anything for him. Besides, he was now in his sixties. In December 1759 Caron signed his "resignation from the business of watchmaking," being succeeded in his workshop, and his window in the rue de Saint-Denis by his son-in-law, Jean-Antoine Lépine, who had worked in Voltaire's watch factory at Ferney and was already known as one of the best watchmakers in the capital. (He had married Caron's daughter Madeleine-Françoise, known as "Fanchon" in the family.)

After a few months of further self-indulgence—"I have dined, I have supped, I have visited, I have solicited"—Beaumarchais wrote to Monsieur Bardin, procureur au Châtelet de Paris, that he had become interested in another royal sinecure, that of grand master of lakes and forests, a post which he could buy for 500,000 livres. Some other grand masters opposed him. Beaumarchais wrote to a minister saying that those officers had objected to his rise to that rank because his father had been "an artist," but, he argued, had not D'Arbonnes, grand master of Orléans, been the son of a hairdresser; Marizy, grand master of Burgundy, son of a clothier; Tellés, grand master of Chalons, son of a Jewish jeweller; and Duvancel, grand master of Paris, son of a button maker? Despite this riposte and the support of the daughters of the king, and of Pâris-Duverney—who wrote that Beaumarchais was a "straightforward young man, with an honest soul, an excellent heart and a cultivated spirit"—he was this time unsuccessful. But a little later, in August 1763, Beaumarchais

Basse-du-Rempart to the splendid 26 rue de Condé, on the left bank near the Palais de Luxembourg, where he bought a large house for 44,000 livres. He installed his father and his two unmarried sisters, Julie ("Bécasse") and Jeanne-Marguerite ("Tonton"), on the third and fourth floors. He himself had two large salons on the *piano nobile,* and on the ground floor were kitchens, as well as a dining room, the last an arrangement relatively rare at that time. Beaumarchais's back windows opened onto the garden of the magnificent Hôtel de Condé; his front windows, on the street, had good iron balconies. Here he began to be "at home" on Fridays to members of the enlightened bourgeoisie and some new nobility. There might be Louis-Auguste Fournier de la Châtaigneraye, an equerry of the queen; the accomplished actor Pierre-Louis Du Bus, known as Préville; and Jeanne Guichonne, Madame Jeanne Henry, a widow with whom Beaumarchais's father fell in love. There would be often as well Jean-Baptiste Octave Janot de Miron, an admirer of Jeanne-Marguerite. Préville, an old friend of the Carons, was to play Figaro in the first production of Beaumarchais's *The Barber of Seville* at the Comédie Française in 1775.

Among those at Beaumarchais's Fridays in 1763 was "a young and beautiful Creole orphan, Pauline Le Breton," who had inherited a rundown property in the rich French colony of Saint-Domingue (now Haiti). She would usually be there escorted by Madame Gaschet, her aunt. Saint-Domingue at that time was the richest colony on earth because of the high price of sugar, which it produced every year in greater quantity. If Beaumarchais could establish that

TWO

A Letter from Madrid

In February 1764 Caron received a bitter letter from his daughter Marie-Josèphe Guilbert, who had been living for more than ten years in Madrid. It read:

> My sister [Lisette] has just been outraged by a man as well accredited as he is dangerous. Twice on the point of marrying her, he has failed in his undertaking and has brusquely withdrawn without even deigning to explain his conduct; the sensibility of my offended sister has thrown her into a deathlike state from which as it appears we shall now not save her. All her nerves are shattered. For six days, she has scarcely opened her mouth. It is such a dishonour that this event has thrown us into a profound depression and I

myself cry night and day, while giving to the unfortunate one consolations which I am not in a sufficiently good state to obtain for myself. All Madrid knows that my sister has nothing with which to reproach herself. If my brother has enough credit to recommend us to the ambassador of France, His Excellency could protect us with a bounty of kindness which would bring an end to the evil which this perfidious person has brought on us, both by his conduct and by his threats.

Lisette at that time was already thirty-three: "on the shelf," as it would be unkindly put in England. Her fiancé, or fiancé manqué, was José Clavijo y Fajardo, a witty, clever, enlightened man of letters originally from the Canary Islands. He loved and admired France. He had recently obtained the sinecure of keeper of the royal archives, which gave him the same kind of position and income which Beaumarchais himself had obtained from the government at Versailles. In 1764 he was thirty-four years old, just two years more than Beaumarchais. He was short, plump, and usually red in the face, rather like an Englishman. But he had always had a great desire to know France. He spoke French. The truth is that he was the kind of man of whom in other circumstances Beaumarchais would—or should—have been an enthusiastic friend. It was later said by gossips that Lisette had for a time been Clavijo's mistress. But in the circumstances of 1760 that would seem improbable. It is an interesting coincidence that one of the seducing villains in *Don*

Quixote has the name of Clavijo too. "Clavijo" would have been a word familiar in Spain since it is a place in the northern province of Logroño where, in the early Middle Ages, a Christian king defeated the Moors allegedly thanks to the miraculous intervention of Saint James.

The patron who had enabled José Clavijo to obtain his advantageous sinecure had been Richard Wall, sprightly conversationalist, a Spanish statesman of Irish origin who had been ambassador in London and then, from 1754 to 1764, secretary of state—in effect chief minister—in Madrid.

It had been understood that Lisette would not marry Clavijo until he became a success. He set about the task of proving himself in a roundabout way. He wanted to produce in Madrid a weekly paper in the style of *The Spectator* of London (or the *Spectateur français,* Marivaux's copy of it in Paris). He obtained enough money to finance just such a journal, which he called *El Pensador.* Marie-Josèphe had told Clavijo sharply, "Begin by succeeding; and when some job, favour of the court, or some other method of living honourably gives you the right to dream of marrying my sister, and if she prefers you to other pretenders to her hand, I shall not refuse my consent." By 1763 he had apparently achieved his aim.

According to Marie-Josèphe, Lisette had refused several good offers of marriage while agreeing to wait for Clavijo. *El Pensador* then became a great success. Clavijo seemed to be interested in everything. Basically an encyclopaedist, in the enlightened French sense of that word, his purpose was to introduce a species of English moralism to Spain. He wrote with brio: a modern French historian of the Spanish enlightenment, Jean Sarrailh, talked of "his customary gaiety." Beaumarchais recorded: "The king himself was amused by this charming production [*El Pensador*], resulting in an atmosphere of benign tolerance towards the author." Clavijo rarely wrote of politics. He would make a minute criticism of such things as bullfighting that, like the king, he disliked. A typical article by him described how a modern Diogenes with his lantern once approached the gilded carriage of an aristocrat. He looked inside and saw—certainly not a human being: "The entire body of this animal was covered in gold paint. It spoke doubloons and spat forth escudos. It was working on genealogy."

Clavijo's best-known essay was probably "The Guide to the Perfect Traveller"—an essay which ironically might have been ideal for Beaumarchais. He wrote in a clear and firm style, without acrimony: "One should not expect refinement in my judgements. My genius is lazy: to translate to paper the idea of the fashion which is presented to me; and, if you insist on precision, entertaining me by correcting or polishing my style, I would renounce the idea of writing rather than subject myself to the heavy business of that labour." He wrote a short play, *La Feria de Valdemoro*, which was produced in 1764. All in all, he was the kind of man of whom in other circumstances Beaumarchais would have strongly approved.

Clavijo had his eccentricities: thus he was curiously hostile to the *autos sacramentales*, religious allegories in the form of plays, which were often acted at the season of Corpus Christi in theatres in the intermissions of substantial plays. (Earlier, they had been performed out of doors on a platform in front of the church of Santa María, or in one of the bigger squares of the capital.) These had their origin in medieval mystery plays but had become profane. Clavijo complained about one such which showed how a company was induced to take the presentation of an old dance—apparently a *chacona*—to the pope for his approval. The pope was represented as saying that he did not think that he could make up his mind without hearing or seeing the dance. At once, the music struck up and, within minutes, the pope and the cardinals had begun to tap their feet, then to sway, and finally to dance with abandon.

Clavijo, a man imbued with the French classicist spirit, affected to be shocked by this playlet. But there was popular backing for it and for other *autos* and, therefore, much criticism of Clavijo's condemnation. Surely he was supporting an official point of view in the hope of gaining further preferment.

Beaumarchais summed up thus the position of Clavijo and his sister in early 1764: "He was promised the first honourable employment at court which became vacant. He outmanoeuvred all other claimants to my sister's hand. . . . The wedding was held back only by the need to wait for the employment which had been promised to this author of pamphlets. At the end of a delay of six years on one side and many cares and kindnesses on the other side, the job appeared and the man vanished." That was Beaumarchais's judgement of the matter, and since he published this account and Clavijo never replied or contradicted him in print, we can assume that it was at least approximately correct.

Beaumarchais continued:

The affair was too well-known for the dénouement to be passed over with indifference. The Carons had already taken a house in Madrid capable of supporting two households. The banns had been published. The outrage shocked all the common friends of the couple, who worked to avenge insult. The ambassador of France became concerned. Then, when Clavijo realised that the French were organising themselves against him, fearing that they could canvas a support which could destroy his entire credit and, in a moment, ruin his rising fortune, he returned to throw himself at the feet of his infuriated fiancée. He did everything he could to recover her affection and, as the high tone of a betrayed woman is usually nothing more than love disguised, everything was soon well organised; the preparations for the marriage began again, the banns were republished, the wedding was announced for three days hence. The reconciliation made as great an impact as the quarrel. On leaving for Saint Ildefonso [La Granja, outside Segovia, where the court went in the summer] to ask permission of his minister to marry, Clavijo said, "My friends, please look after the wavering heart of my mistress until I return from the palace and make all the arrangements so that on my return I can take her to church."

[Clavijo] returned [to Madrid] the following day; but instead of escorting his victim to the altar, he told the poor wretch that he had changed his mind a second time; the outraged friends went immediately to him; the insolent fellow had no defence and said that they were all trying to damage him, and that the French were seeking to torment him. . . . On receiving the news, the young French girl fell again into the convulsions which made people fear for her life.

Caron in Versailles gave Beaumarchais the letter from Marie-Josèphe. He said "Look, my son, these two sad ladies are no less your sisters than the other ones here."

Beaumarchais said: "Alas, father, what kind of recommendation can I obtain for them? What can I ask for them? Who knows if they have not made some mistakes which they hide from us with the shame which today envelops them?"

The Spanish court was usually at La Granja in July and August; Clavijo's change of heart must have come soon after that date. But it was only in February that Madame Guilbert wrote her letter. It must be that the sisters in Madrid decided to inform their family in Paris only when all help nearer at hand had failed.

Beaumarchais was especially struck by the phrase of his father which sought to remind him that these ladies in Madrid were no less sisters than the others in Paris though they had been away so long: "Don't weep," he told his father,

> I am going to do something which will astonish you but which seems to me the wisest course. My eldest sister has mentioned several respectable people in Paris who will vouch for the good conduct and the virtues of her own flesh and blood. I shall see them and, if their testimony makes her out as honourable as the French ambassador in Madrid does, I shall ask for leave [from Versailles], I shall set off and, only bearing in mind the need for prudence and my own sensitivity, I shall have vengeance on the traitor or bring them [my sisters] back to Paris where they can perhaps share with us my own modest fortune.

Beaumarchais told his "august protectresses"—the princesses, daughters of the king—that "a very sad affair demands my presence in Madrid." When they asked him to be precise, he showed them the letter from his eldest sister. "Partez et soyez sage," one of them thereupon said—Leave and be sensible—adding, "You will not lack for support in Spain if your conduct is reasonable." Presumably that meant that the French government could be counted on to help.

This account leaves out one essential item: that "on the rebound," as it were, Lisette accepted a proposal of marriage from Jean Durand, a French businessman who lived in Madrid and in some ways was perhaps a more suitable match for her than Clavijo. That did not modify Caron's distress, nor his son's plan. Beaumarchais wrote to Durand on February 7, 1764, to say that he was not in favour of the marriage unless it could be shown radically to improve his sister's lot.

This is an obscure chapter in the curiously complex history of Beaumarchais's treatment of his sister. Durand seems to have been a conventional businessman who would do anything to please the Beaumarchais family. No doubt he, like so many, was mesmerised by Beaumarchais's charm and successes.

Early in April 1764 Beaumarchais told the Duc de Choiseul, the French minister of foreign affairs, that family matters were obliging him to undertake a journey to Spain. He explained that Madame Victoire—one of the princesses—thought the journey necessary. On April 7 he received "royal permission to be in Spain for six months on matters which particularly concerned him." This brevet was signed by the king and his minister, the Comte de Saint-Florentin, who had upheld Beaumarchais's case in the affair of the "échappement."

The foreign minister, Choiseul, also approved. He was a delightful, cultivated, easygoing individual: "Never has there been a minister so indiscreet as M. de Choiseul," wrote, rather severely, the Danish ambassador, the German baron de Gleichen. "It was his main weakness; his lightness of touch, the strength of his wit, his taste for jokes, and often the effervescence of his temper were its natural causes. But," he added, struggling to be fair, "never have I met a man who has better known how to spread such a mood of happiness and contentment around him. When he goes into a room, he seems to look into his pockets and take out of them an unquenchable abundance of jokes and gaiety."

Some other charming impressions recorded of Choiseul in the life of Madame de Pompadour by the Goncourt brothers somewhat recall England in the age of the cabinet of Harold Macmillan. Casanova wrote of him: "He never paid his creditors and never disturbed his debtors. He was generous: a lover of art and artists to whom he liked to be of service, and what they did for him he looked upon as a grateful offering. He was an intellectual but hated all detail and minute research, being of a naturally indolent and procrastinatory disposition. His favourite saying was 'There's plenty of time for that.'" He was loved by his wife but was continually unfaithful to her. Some have therefore seen Choiseul as an inspiration for Beaumarchais's Count of Almaviva in his plays. But Almaviva was not a politician.

Beaumarchais naturally talked about his plans to his financial friend, his devoted supporter, the imaginative and inventive Pâris-Duverney. The latter was, we suppose, mildly touched by the formal reasons for the journey. But he had other more mercenary ideas. In Spain there were many opportunities. Perhaps Beaumarchais could arrange, first, to obtain for him and thus for France the much coveted licence to sell slaves to the Spanish empire, which was at that time open to purchase; second, perhaps he could establish the right of a monopoly for a French company to trade for twenty years in Louisiana—the vast, empty colony in North America which had in 1762 been secretly transferred from France to Spain; third, there was a possibility of securing the right to provide the food for the Spanish army; and, fourth, he might obtain the contract to colonise the Sierra Morena, the deserted mountains which lay between Castile and Andalusia and which, Pâris-Duverney had heard, might be made into a pilot plan for a rural economy.

Pâris-Duverney said to Beaumarchais: "Of course, go and save the life of your sister. As for the [other] affairs with which you are charged, whatever you discover, remember that I constitute your support. I have promised the royal family [to do it] and I will never fail a sacred engagement such as that." Presumably this was a reference to the license to sell slaves. Pâris-Duverney gave Beaumarchais the large sum of 200,000 francs in notes payable to the bearer for his expenses.

At the same time, Caron, Beaumarchais's father, had his own financial interest in his son's journey; he wanted him to try and recover money owed him by grandees or their wives who had bought watches or clocks from him. That most grandees in Spain possessed two watches had, of course, helped his sales. The debtors were mostly important people: they included the Condesa-Duquesa de Benavente, the Duquesa de Bournonville, the Condesa de Uceda, the young but ruined Marquis de Castelar, the old Catalan merchant Miguel Ferrer, and the Condesa de Fuenclara. The last named lady had been a friend of Caron's in her youth and would play a part in Beaumarchais's life in Madrid, whatever happened to the debts to his father.

THREE

A Journey to Spain

Beaumarchais set off for Spain. At that time, journeys of that kind were unusual and were not embarked upon lightly. Beaumarchais had not hurried his departure, contrary to his later claim that he had dropped everything and left abruptly to save his sister. Nor on the journey itself did he seem in haste, for he stopped for a day or two at Tours, at Bordeaux, and at Bayonne, respectively. Probably the reasons for these stops were commercial: Pâris-Duverney needed good wood from southwest France to sell as *parquet* in great houses in Paris. At Bayonne, Beaumarchais had an accident spoken of by Pauline Le Breton, but the nature of the experience remains a mystery. (She added that this was an "unworthy journey which displeases me, Good God.") In a letter to Madrid, Beaumarchais's patron in Versailles, the Duc de la Vallière, commiserated with him about his "bad night which you spent in the Landes of Bordeaux, but I hope that it will not have consequences." It did not. What could have happened? Beaumarchais was always getting into difficulties in those days. An armed conflict is quite possible.

Beaumarchais hired at Bayonne a valet, "a *mestizo* who was a fourth part Spanish and three parts Indian," who in Madrid was to steal his wallet and flee. He was also joined in southwest France by Périer, a French merchant who pretended to have business in Madrid but had been persuaded by Caron in Paris to protect his son on the journey.

A travelling companion in the last stages of Beaumarchais's journey to Madrid was the Marquis d'Aubarède—that is, Guillaume-Claude d'Aubarède, Comte de Laval, Baron de Chamousset, an adventurer then in his middle forties. He had been a soldier to begin with, becoming lieutenant du roi at Belfort. He had then been imprisoned in the Bastille in 1762 for making slanderous threats against la Vicomtesse de Noé. He fled to northern Spain, where he sought to gain the confidence of Beaumarchais and therefore perhaps be named governor of Louisiana if the plans of Pâris-Duverney and Beaumarchais were to mature happily. He was one of the many curious adventurers who are to be found in the records of those days, flitting easily between capitals in the hope of profit and advancement.

Beaumarchais did not record what he saw on his journey through the mountainous Basque country and the flat plain of northern Castile, which he crossed on the way to Madrid. But he assuredly would have seen in the towns through which he had to pass the extent to which there was one major difference in Spain from France: an elaborate cult of the Virgin. Most travellers noticed that in the eighteenth century. All the way down through old Castile, Beaumarchais would have seen surprising signs of how the Virgin was looked upon as the patron of the kingdom in a way which was never the case in France. At that time, every Spaniard looked on the Virgin as a friend who was constantly concerned only about him and who dreamed of his happiness. Casanova, travelling along much the same route a year or two later, thought that the Pyrenees were "the most picturesque, fertile, and agreeable" mountains in Europe. But he was shocked to find that the roads seemed to vanish altogether twenty leagues south of them: "There were steep ascents and violent descents but no traces of carriage wheels, and so it was throughout the whole of old Castile."

Beaumarchais and his party arrived in the Spanish capital on May 18, 1764. They would have entered through the old Puerta de Alcalá, in much the same place as its successor, built in the 1780s, and then consisting of a large central gate and a smaller one on each side. Above the central arch a statue of Our Lady de las Mercedes looked down and, by her side, were smaller ones, of the Beata Marina de Jesús and of San Pedro Nolasco. This old gate was one of about ten similar ones in the city, each set in mud walls in poor condition. Contraband passed easily as a result into Madrid, despite the customs police installed at short intervals in cabins along the wall whose purpose was to impose irritating local taxes.

The moment of Beaumarchais's arrival was the third day of the fiesta of San Isidro, the patron saint of Madrid. The celebrated pilgrimage to the hermitage of San Isidro, the labourer-saint, on the south side of the city, would already have occurred on the first day. Those who went to the hermitage might drink from the miraculous water. They assuredly also picnicked there, as Goya's famous painting a generation later delightfully showed. The hermitage was renowned for the sparkling water from the fountain near the chapel and which was said to have been miraculously found by San Isidro himself when digging there. In 1528 the nearly fatal illness of the infant Philip (later King Philip II) was allegedly cured by water from this fount. Philip's mother, the Empress Isabella, therefore had a chapel built beside the fountain.

The king in Spain in 1764 was Charles III, the third son of King Philip V, the first Spanish Bourbon on the Spanish throne. Charles was much marked by his powerful Italian mother, Elizabeth Farnese, the queen mother, who, if half-blind, was still alive in Madrid and still to be reckoned with. She was by then, however, more concerned with her collection of more than 1,600 fans than with power.

Charles's own successful twenty years as king of Naples (1739–1759) had also affected him. His wife, María Amalia, daughter of the agreeable if indolent King Augustus III of Saxony, had died at thirty-six in 1760 soon after reaching her new kingdom. She had been a domineering personage and, in Naples, Charles had seemed to do her bidding. He had had no *adventure amoureuse* since her death, though; instead, he had been consumed by "boredom, that infirmity of all monarchs," as Beaumarchais put it.

The king was said to have specifically arranged his day so as to avoid physical temptations. Thus he rose at seven and had his hair dressed. At eight, he heard Mass, drank chocolate, and took snuff. At nine, he saw his ministers and worked with them till eleven. Then he dined (alone) and set out to hunt at twelve. At seven in the evening he had a light supper wherever he was, and, at eight, he returned home to the palace, often so tired that he fell asleep before he undressed.

Charles was "of a complete ugliness," recalled the Baron Glei-chen, "from head to toe, if without any deformity." He added: "One became used to this ugliness because of his air of benevolence and the simple and natural good manners which accompanied it and which he had instead of grace. The king had an air of bonhomie so original that one would have liked to have shown respect for him for that reason alone." Beaumarchais met the king later and found him "a limited man isolated by his general mistrust and tormented above all by that fear of being dominated which is such a powerful emotion with weak spirits, and which left everyone who approached him lacking in any power to make decisions. His ministers, with an appearance of despotism which they impose on fools, are with him no more than timid valets before a master as mistrustful as he is ab-solute. His favourites sustain their credit only by doing nothing."

One man alone, Beaumarchais thought, was really influential: Américo Pini, "his dear *valet de chambre,* the sole person to whom the king dares to open his soul, with whom he passes all his days, shut up ten hours out of twenty-four. It is from this man, as important as he is obscure, that I acquired my best knowledge of this prince. But apart from the ministers, Pini, and sometimes, in respect of religious matters, his confessor, there is no one who dares speak of anything to the king." All the same King Charles III was renowned as one of Europe's "enlightened despots"; and he deserved the adjective without seeming despotic.

Beaumarchais, after being in Madrid for several months, came to think that there was no country in the world where the government was as powerful as it was in Spain. "As there is no intermediate authority between the minister and the people which tempers the activity of the legislative and executive power, it seems that abuse must often be on the side of government. However there is no prince which uses his limitless power more soberly than the king of Spain; being able to decide everything by a single word." Yet events were soon to show that, in France, a similar lack of intermediate authorities would ruin the old system of government.

The buildings which King Charles inspired in Madrid are splendid: they included the museum of natural history, which is now the Museo del Prado; the church of San Francisco; a new gate of Alcalá; the palace of postal services (Palacio de Correos) in the Puerta del Sol; and the customs house (Aduana) in the noble Calle Alcalá. The king also inspired the beautiful fountains in the Paseo del Prado, from that of Cibeles to that of his ancestor the Emperor Charles V in front of the hermitage of Atocha, and including Neptune. King

Charles III was thus nicknamed Madrid's best mayor. He had previously been Naples's most successful monarch, responsible there for the lovely royal palace of Capodimonte as well as the elegant Teatro San Carlo.

Yet Charles's character was austere. His best-known remark was "Rain breaks no bones," signifying his intention to hunt every day; and his best-known portrait, by Goya, about twenty years later than the time of Beaumarchais's visit, shows him out shooting. His most important achievement in the capital was to make it cleaner. He also put lights in the streets. Beaumarchais was astonished at the opposition with which the king met: "Cities are like children. They weep when they are scrubbed and cleaned," he wrote; and he commented a little later, "The determination of the reigning prince to clean up the city has conquered the obstinate desire of the Spaniards to live surrounded by dung, so this city is becoming one of the cleanest places which I have ever seen, well opened up, adorned by numerous squares and public fountains in truth more useful to the people than agreeable to a man of taste, while a lively and appetising air circulates through the city with ease."

The most important of Charles III's ministers in 1764 was Jerónimo Grimaldi, Marqués de Grimaldi, minister of foreign affairs, then in his forties, who had the name of being a great friend of France (though Beaumarchais thought that he did not deserve that reputation). Like Choiseul in France, he was a very easygoing and agreeable man, for whom good manners sometimes seemed a substitute for intelligence. Born in Genoa, in a great mercantile family concerned in Spanish commerce since the fifteenth century, he had come to Spain early in life and had held several diplomatic posts, including that of ambassador in Paris, before becoming foreign minister in Madrid. He had in 1761 been responsible for the famous Family Pact, which sought to unite the foreign policies of the Bourbons in Spain and France. Beaumarchais later wrote that he was "lazy and notably unenlightened, having only a feeble talent for measuring the views of those narrow souls shut up in their economic work." But that comment reflected the disappointments which Beaumarchais sustained in consequence of dealing with him. The historian Albert Sorel considered him a philosopher. In effect, he was prime minister of Spain at this time, though the title did not exist.

More important in terms of real power was a Sicilian, Leopoldo de Gregorio, Marqués de Squillace (sometimes spelled Esquilache). He was minister of finance, having held the same post with Charles in Naples. He was efficient, competent, and liberal but, like a surprising number of enlightened men, cold, impersonal, and inhuman. Beaumarchais thought him "an old calculator, an extortioner grown white in adding up obscure combinations of interests, who uses his ascendancy over the king to keep Grimaldi from expressing his views." De Gregorio was to meet much difficulty when, in the interests of security in the street, he tried to modernise Spanish dress a year or two later by abolishing full-length cloaks.

Julián de Arriaga was the minister of marine in Madrid and also responsible for the American empire. A sailor by profession and a Basque by blood, he had been governor-general of Venezuela, and there he had gained golden opinions for tact. He had already been a minister for ten years and would continue to be so for another twelve. For Beaumarchais, he was "a man who counted for nothing: as simple as he was devout and as little educated." He hated the French. It had been he who had to tell the king of the fall of Havana in the recent war against the English, and it was said that he had not yet recovered from that humiliation. He was in charge of maintaining the large Spanish fleet which had to defend the coasts of both Spain and the empire in time of war and escort the famous galleons which carried the precious metals from the American mines to Europe. But the navy which set out to guarantee the state's wealth absorbed much of it.

These men were the senior ministers. Junior to them, but already pressing them for a place in the bright sun of royal favour, were a group of more determinedly progressive men: Floridablanca, Aranda, Campomanes, and subsequently Jovellanos, men with rational ideas who would seek to introduce radical change in Spain in the later 1760s and 1770s. There were also such "enlightened" proconsuls as the Asturian Conde de Revillagigedo, the Flemish Marqués de Croix, and the Irish-born General Alejandro O'Reilly, who were ready to enact in the empire what had been agreed in Madrid. The Spanish empire in the 1760s was not badly managed. But those clever men still in the wings would in the end create confusion by their well-meant reforms so that the early days of the reign of King Charles III when Beaumarchais was in Madrid would seem to many a golden age.

FOUR

Clavijo

In Madrid, Beaumarchais seemed immediately at home. On his
arrival, he naturally went to his sisters in their house above their
shop "of frivolities" in the Calle de la Montera, which, then as now,
runs down into the Puerta del Sol, in the very centre of the city,
from the north. It is today one of the shabbiest of streets. But in the
eighteenth century, it was elegant as well as lively. There was a popular inn, the Mesón de la Herradura, on the right-hand pavement on
the way up to the Red de San Luis. There was a good bookshop, too,
the Luna, where one could also buy flutes. A nineteenth-century
dramatist, Narciso Serra, was to write:

> *Que si usiría viniera*
> *Aquí de alcalde menor,*

Al corte le dijera
Que es mucha calle, señor,
La Calle de la Montera.

If your lordship were coming
Here as local magistrate
To anyone from the court you'd say
It's a real street, sir,
The Calle de la Montera

Beaumarchais found his sisters surrounded by friends, to whom "the warmth" of his resolution had given the desire to meet him. He himself thought, though, that his sister had gained an unfortunate reputation from her dealings with Clavijo which might damage his own negotiations with the court of Spain about the various plans of Pâris-Duverney. That was a serious matter. Could he, or France, lose these possibilities just because of Lisette? He thought nevertheless: "It's necessary first and foremost to recover the honour of Lisette." And so he said to those assembled in the Caron sisters' house: "Do not be astonished if I use these first moments which I spend with you to learn the exact truth of this unfortunate adventure. I beg you, honest people who surround me, whom I regard as my friends since you are my sisters' friends, not to allow the slightest inexactitude to go uncorrected. For to serve you, it's essential that I am very accurately informed."

The story he heard was long and, of course, revolved around the extraordinary conduct of Clavijo. But Lisette's feelings were obviously as much those of hurt pride as of love. Indeed, as we have seen, she had been planning to marry the businessman who had worked with Caron in Paris, Jean Durand. At the end of the story as told to him, Beaumarchais embraced Lisette and said, "Now I know everything. Calm yourself. I see with pleasure that you are not in love with this man. My conduct will therefore be more relaxed. Only tell me where I can find him in Madrid."

Everyone advised Beaumarchais not to seek Clavijo in Madrid but to go first to greet the French ambassador at Aranjuez, where the Spanish court stayed from Easter till the beginning of the summer. It was a little more than thirty miles south of Madrid, or about a day's ride of ten hours, in an oasis famous in the spring for its strawberries.

Hemingway would one day write well of that fruit: "Coming from the hot sun of the bare, desert country suddenly under the shade of the trees, [you] see brown-armed girls with baskets of fresh strawberries piled on the smooth, bare, cool ground, strawberries you cannot reach around with thumb and forefinger, damp and cool, packed on green leaves in wicker baskets."

The building of the palace and the park at Aranjuez had been the work of King Philip II in the second half of the sixteenth century. Many of the trees to be seen in the 1760s had been planted by Philip's Flemish gardeners. The park was characterised by lush lawns and shaded walks. There was also a herb garden, and the rose garden once proudly produced 5,400 pounds of rose petals. There are many charming references to the place in the literature of the court.

Remember the first lines of Schiller's magnificent, if historically rather misleading, *Don Carlos:*

> *The happy days at Aranjuez*
> *Are now at their end.*

All the friends of Lisette hoped Beaumarchais would go first and see the French ambassador, whose well-known prudence they thought should direct his own actions, for "the enemy" was well established in powerful places. They thought that Beaumarchais should do nothing in Madrid before calling on His Excellency in Aranjuez.

Beaumarchais reported that he replied: "That's a good idea, my friends, for so I regard you, only arrange a vehicle for the journey and I shall go and greet the ambassador at court. But do not take it ill if, before going to see him, I make some essential plans; the only way in which you can all serve me is to keep the secret of my arrival until my return from Aranjuez."

But Beaumarchais did several things before setting out for Aranjuez: first, he sought to establish an understanding with one of the many French bankers then in Madrid, Drouillet, "an estimable man," as he first thought, though his wife had "absurd airs." Later, disillusioned, he wrote that Drouillet "is a Jew and that's all there is to be said."

His second action seems to have been to hire four secretary-translators. He did not want to be outmanoeuvred by any eventualities that derived from his lack of fluency in Spanish.

Third, he had some conversation with his sister Lisette about her matrimonial plans, extraordinarily inconvenient in the circumstances, with Jean Durand; and he must have counselled her, instructed her perhaps, not to pursue that idea for the time being.

Finally, he did seek out Clavijo: "I took a suit out of my suitcase, put it on and . . . went to the house of Don José Clavijo." Where this was is not evident. But Madrid was then a small city, and the Calle de la Montera, in which the Caron sisters lived, was, as we have seen, central. The route, wherever Clavijo had his dwelling, would have been through streets bordered mostly by single-storey houses—"*casas de malicia,*" they were called—for two or more storeys entailed a tax. Beaumarchais would have found that, unlike the houses of Paris, the majority of buildings still had no panes of glass in their small windows, for such were thought too expensive. Houses had not been numbered until 1750; they were still usually known by the name of the resident. Even in 1764 they were identified by a number within a block (*manzana*). Nor were the narrow streets often paved; frequently they were covered with mud. Where there was paving, a gutter ran down the centre of the way. Such thoroughfares were rough. A peasant girl in one of Ramón de la Cruz's playlets (*sainetes*) described how, before arriving in Madrid, she had supposed that the streets would be covered with soft cushions; instead, they seemed "paved with daggers."

There was also, despite the good intentions of the present king, much refuse in every street. House doors were still often used by passers-by who needed to relieve themselves. Dogs and even pigs wandered freely. Cleaning was still confined to the so-called *marea,* a word which would usually be translated "the tide": at night a group of carts fitted with low revolving beams would scoop up the heavier rubbish. Torchbearers would precede them, and a group of men would follow with brooms. This "pestiferous procession" caused much dust, and distress, especially to returning partygoers.

Beaumarchais's first impression of the city is unclear, except that he thought the sky wonderful. That is a frequent reaction. Jovellanos, the enlightened judge and economist, when he arrived from Seville a few years later, wrote that the place was so dominated by religion that he felt stifled:

> The capital has more churches than houses, more priests than laymen, and more altars than kitchens; even in the filthy house entrances, even in the vile taverns, one can see small altarpieces, a medley of wax articles, small basins of water, and religious lamps. One can hardly take a step without meeting some brotherhood or procession, or an assemblage of people reciting the rosary as they march, brayings of the subchanters and the sacred jargon of the musicians entertaining devout souls with *villancicos,* carols or couplets in praise of the Virgin. Even the most recondite mysteries of religion are sung by blind men at tavern doors to the admittedly agreeable and majestic accompaniment of the guitar. Every corner is covered with announcements of novenas, and at every other corner

there are sold accounts of miracles as credible as Ovid's *Metamorphoses.*

A French traveller might have found the vegetables of Spain superior to those of France, but milk and butter were almost un-obtainable. Most Spanish kitchens were unable to bake or roast anything substantial; turkey, rabbit, pigeon, geese, and much fish were sent to the large ovens of professional pastry cooks.

Beaumarchais might have gone to Clavijo's in a sedan chair; but it is more likely that he would have walked, down the Calle de la Montera, perhaps past people being carefully deloused in the street by their relations, then through the semicircular Puerta del Sol, which was at that time considerably smaller, as well as more ele-gant, than it is now. The fashionable church of Buen Suceso domi-nated the corner of the square between the streets San Jerónimo and Alcalá. That place of worship itself seemed to be thronged by praying prostitutes, pious pickpockets, and talkative friars. Many swindlers to be found there would promise fortunes in return for a pittance. They jostled at the entrance for attention with blind ballad singers and even with "abbés," those mysterious noncleri-cal clergymen who often acted as professional letter writers. This church was razed in the 1830s, and now the many-mirrored Hotel Paris stands in its place.

In front of the church there was a much-loved fountain known as the Mariblanca, surmounted by a statue of Venus. A song insisted,

Whoever seeks a wife,
A maiden pure and silent,
May hie him to the square,
For there is Mariblanca.

Beaumarchais could hardly have failed to have seen there, dipping their pitchers in the water, one or two water carriers, who were often in those days Gallegos—natives of the only part of Spain where lack of rain did not constitute a problem.

There were also then in the Puerta del Sol two monasteries, first that of San Felipe el Real, with its spacious porch or platform, just at the beginning of the Calle Mayor; and, second, that of Nuestra Señora de la Victoria, at the entrance to the Calle San Jerónimo. The porch of San Felipe was known as the "Gradas" (the steps) or "el Mentidero" (the house of lies), a place where people gossipped and argued. Beneath it were thirty-four small toy shops known as the *covachuelas*, cellars, usually crowded with children examining wooden horses or some expensive new German toy. The Convento de La Victoria, on the north side of the square, had been founded to commemorate the great Spanish victory of Lepanto against the Turkish navy in 1571.

The tallest building in the Puerta del Sol in 1764 was a foundling hospital which lay between the calles Carmen and Preciados. A troop of soldiers was at that time established on its ground floor.

If Beaumarchais was in the Puerta del Sol between 1 and 2 o'clock in the afternoon, he might have caught the engaging sight

of one or two *petimetres,* dandies, gabbling for an elegant minute or two a few Italian or French phrases which they might not
even understand before teetering into the church of Buen Suceso
for a prayer. ("What will they think of me tomorrow in the Buen
Suceso?" asks a petimetre in Ramón de la Cruz's play *La Devoción
Engañosa,* after a night out on the eve of Saint John, June 23.)
There were also the even more exquisite *currutacos,* superdandies
whose steps would be more measured, and who could be seen taking snuff—perhaps prepared with foreign-made rose vinegar—in a
refined manner. The currutaco's hair would be exquisitely powdered,
and he would be seen "swinging himself along on his toes like a
tightrope dancer, swaying to and fro as if he were drunk, offending
the nostrils of passers-by with the scent of his ointments, his oils,
and his perfume." The twenty-first century cannot approach the
exquisite charm of these glittering fantasists.

When Beaumarchais reached the house of Clavijo, he found
that that writer was out, having gone, so the housekeeper said, to the
house where a certain lady was holding a salon—a *tertulia,* as the
Spaniards would have had it, the word being a remote homage to
the Latin author Tertullian, whom it had been fashionable to quote
in Madrid in the sixteenth century. A tertulia meant, in the 1760s, a
gathering of individuals for the purpose of conversation, usually in
a private house. There might also be games, some dancing (in the
wintertime, in particular), even gambling, and some refreshments.
The hostess would often receive her guests seated cross-legged on a
cushion on a dais covered with a carpet. Sometimes this *estrado,* as it

was known, would be cut off from the rest of the room by a railing, and sometimes there would be a canopy over it. Occasionally, there might be málaga wine for the men and iced water or punch for the ladies. Sometimes there would be an *ambigú*, a light buffet. Otherwise, there was little social life in Madrid. Beaumarchais would later tell his patron in Paris, the Duc de la Vallière, "As everyone lives at home, except for assemblies called tertulias, which are more throngs of people than social gatherings . . . the great lords are almost only known by their families."

Beaumarchais went to the house where Clavijo had been invited and, without giving his name, sent up a message saying that he had just come from France, with some presents for him. He was eager to see him even though they had never met. Clavijo agreed to such an encounter, without knowing who he was, for chocolate at 9 o'clock the following morning. Clavijo assumed that anyone from France would welcome that concoction of sugar, cinnamon, and chocolate mixed with hot water which was the usual drink for breakfast of the Spanish upper and middle classes in those days: the chocolate being an imperial import from Bolivia, Mexico, Peru, or Venezuela.

Next day, May 19, 1764, Beaumarchais was at Clavijo's lodgings at half-past eight. He was with his "travelling companion," the Marquis d'Aubarède. He found Clavijo in a splendid house which belonged to a certain Don José Antonio de Portugués, "one of the most esteemed of the heads of bureau of the ministry [of foreign affairs] and so much a friend of Clavijo that he allowed him to use his house whenever he liked as if it were his own." Portugués, then in his fifties, was himself a writer who had encountered a modest success.

We should imagine the house being large and at night lit by chandeliers; there would have been little furniture, and what chairs there were would have been low. The walls might have been whitewashed, though wallpaper was already coming in that year, as Ramón de la Cruz's play, *El Petimetre,* suggests.

According to his own account (and we have to recall that we have no other), Beaumarchais sailed into an attack on Clavijo with tremendous energy and aplomb. He spoke in French, a language which he had by now discovered that Clavijo spoke well. "I am charged, sir," he said, "by a French society of men of letters to organise in all the towns I pass through a literary correspondence with the most learned men of the country. As no Spaniard has written better than the author of *El Pensador,* to whom I have the honour to speak now and whose literary merit has been attested by the king and so confided to him the supervision of one of his archives, I have thought it impossible to serve my friends better than by connecting them with a man of your merit."

Clavijo must have been pleased at this elaborate introduction. Then Beaumarchais described the circumstances of his sister's difficulties, but not revealing that he knew the people in the story until he said, "This story moved the heart of the brother of those sisters to the point that he asked for a holiday from his duties in Versailles to come here to throw light on the complicated matter.

He has done no less than make a sudden journey from Paris to Madrid. And that brother, it is I," thundered Beaumarchais, "who have left everything, country, duty, family, state, pleasures to avenge an innocent and unhappy sister; it is I who come armed with legal backing and with determination to unmask a traitor, to paint his soul in blood on his face; and that traitor, it is you!"

This speech was much the most famous which Beaumarchais ever made. Again, we must assume that it was close to what Beaumarchais said, though surely the account gained something in the telling.

The unfortunate Clavijo tried to make apologies, but Beaumarchais said firmly, "Do not interrupt me, sir; you have nothing to say to me and much to hear. To begin with, have the goodness to declare before my friend who has come express from France with me to be present if by some lack of faith, some lightness of spirit, some kind of feebleness, or bitterness, or some other vice whatever it may be, my sister has deserved the double outrage which you have had the cruelty to impose publicly upon her."

"No, sir, I recognise Doña María your sister as a lady full of spirit, grace, and virtues."

"She has given you reason to complain of her since you first knew her?"

"Never, never."

"And why then, monster that you are," Beaumarchais asked, getting up from his chair, "have you had the barbarity to take her to death's door only because she preferred you to ten others more honest and richer than you?"

"Ah monsieur . . . if you only knew."

"That's enough!" Then, turning to his companion, d'Aubarède, Beaumarchais said, "You have heard this recognition of the innocence of my sister; go and publish it. The rest of what I have to say to Monsieur does not require witnesses." D'Aubarède accordingly left. Beaumarchais then said, "Now that we are alone, here is my proposal, and I hope you will approve it." Clavijo took a deep breath. Then Beaumarchais went on:

It suits us both, for different reasons, that you do not marry my sister. And you must realise that I do not come here to play the heavy part of a brother in a play who wants his sister to marry. But all the same, you have outraged at your pleasure a woman of honour because you imagined her without support in a foreign country; that proceeding is that of a dishonest man and a coward.

So you must then begin by recognising in a letter in your own handwriting in full liberty of action, with your doors open and all your friends in the room, though they will not understand us, because we are speaking in French, that you are an abominable man who has deceived and betrayed my sister . . . and with your declaration in my hand, I shall leave for Aranjuez, where my ambassador is. I shall show him the declaration, I shall immediately have it printed; the day after tomorrow the court and the city will be inundated with the news of it; for I have strong backing here, and time and money too. All this will be employed to ensure that you lose your place at court, to pursue you in such a way and without remorse until my sister's resentment is appeased and until she says "stop" to me.

"I shall not make such a declaration," said Clavijo.

Beaumarchais said, "I can well believe it because perhaps in your place I would not do so either. But here is the reverse side of the medal. Write or do not write. But from this moment I shall stay with you. I shall never leave you alone. I shall go wherever you go until the time when, exhausted by our proximity, you will meet me behind the Buen Retiro."

The Buen Retiro is the palace on the east side of Madrid built by King Philip III in the early seventeenth century and used by the king whenever he was in Madrid. The allusion to this venue was a challenge to a duel. "If I am more fortunate than you," Beaumarchais said, "I, without seeing my ambassador, without speaking to anyone here, shall take my dying sister in my arms, place her in a chaise, and return with her to France. If, on the contrary, fortune favours you, all will have been already said by me; I made my will before leaving Paris, you will have had all the advantage over us, and you can allow yourself to laugh at our expense. Please send up breakfast."

Clavijo rang the bell. A lackey entered, bringing chocolate. While Beaumarchais took his cup, Clavijo walked up and down in silence. Eventually he said: "Monsieur de Beaumarchais, listen to me. Nothing in the world can excuse my conduct towards your sister. Ambition has ruined me; but if I had known that Doña María had a brother such as you, far from looking on her as a lonely foreigner, I would have realised the great advantages to me which would follow our marriage."

This remarkably honest if cynical statement made an impression on Beaumarchais, whose motives for being in Spain were, as we know, much more mixed than he was making out.

Clavijo went on: "You have inspired in me the highest esteem for you, and I place myself at your feet in order to beg you to repair, if it is still possible, all the damage which I have done your sister. Give her back to me, dear sir. And I shall believe myself too happy to receive my wife from you and also a pardon for all my crimes."

"There is no more time," said Beaumarchais. "My sister does not love you any more. Only make the declaration, that is all I ask of you. And you will find afterwards that it is a good thing that as a declared enemy I avenge my sister as her feelings dictate to me."

Beaumarchais then made Clavijo sign a declaration which he had previously written. It read:

I, the undersigned José Clavijo, keeper of one of the archives of the Crown, recognise that, having been received with kindness in the household of Madame Guilbert, I deceived Mademoiselle Caron, her sister, by the honourable promise which I made and repeated a thousand times to marry her, which I have failed to do, without any fault or inadequacy on her part being able to serve as a pretext or excuse for my lack of faith; on the contrary, the wisdom of this lady for whom I have the most profound respect, has always been unqualified and without a stain. I recognise that, by my conduct, by the superficiality of my comments, and by the interpretation which could be made, I have openly outraged this virtuous lady to whom I ask pardon by this statement, which is made freely and of my own will. . . . I promise any other kind of reparation which she may desire if this one is not suitable for her. Done at Madrid.

Beaumarchais took this paper and said: "I am not a cowardly enemy, sir; it is without any special commission that I come to avenge my sister. I have warned you of it. Take pride in yourself for having avoided the cruel use which I was going to make of the weapon with which you provided me."

"Monsieur," remarkably returned Clavijo, "I believe myself to be talking to the most offended, but most generous, of men; before defaming me, grant me time in which I can try and recover Doña María. It was in that spirit alone that I have signed the apology which you were demanding. But before presenting myself, I have resolved to charge someone to plead my case with her. And that someone is you."

"I shall have nothing to do with it," Beaumarchais replied.

"At least tell her," said Clavijo, "the bitter remorse which you have observed in me. I restrict my requests to that. If you refuse, I shall commission someone else to place myself at her feet."

Beaumarchais promised him that he would do as he asked.

The return of d'Aubarède to the house of Marie-Josèphe and Lisette had meantime created alarm in the Calle de la Montera. But as soon as Beaumarchais also came back to describe what had happened, and as soon as they saw the declaration which Clavijo had signed, cries of joy broke out, and tears were succeeded by embraces. Everyone had a different point of view to express, for some thought that it was right to pardon Clavijo, others thought that he should be condemned, and everyone talked at the same time. But Lisette cried out: "No, never, never will I speak to him. Let my brother hasten to Aranjuez, go and see Monsieur the ambassador; everything is there: take your decisions on his advice."

Before going to the court at Aranjuez, Beaumarchais wrote to Clavijo to say that his sister had not wanted to hear a single word in his favour. Clavijo in return begged Beaumarchais to come and see him again, and Beaumarchais went happily. After a thousand imprecations against himself, his demands were limited to obtaining permission that, during Beaumarchais's brief absence in Aranjuez, Clavijo, with a common friend, would go to speak with Marie-Josèphe. Beaumarchais said to him, "I will make your dishonour public if on my return you have not obtained her pardon."

Honour! We should recall at this moment the words of the great historian Burckhardt that, much more than religion, honour was for a long time "the decisive rule of conduct [in European civilisation] . . . that enigmatic mixture of conscience and egotism which often survives in modern man after he has lost, whether by his own fault or not, faith, love, and hope." The word *honour* was constantly then on the lips of all well-educated people, and those who aspired to such a qualification thought continuously of it.

Then at last Beaumarchais went to Aranjuez to show the declaration which he had wrung from Clavijo to the French ambassador. This was Pierre-Paul Ossun, Baron de Helches et Saint-Luc, "a man of magnetism"—*grande allure*—who knew Voltaire and corresponded with him on the subject so close to Beaumarchais's head if not his heart, namely, watches, which Voltaire intended to have produced in workshops financed by himself at Ferney. In Madrid, Ossun had also arranged for Voltaire's tragedy *Tancrède,* a play produced in 1760, to be performed in his embassy. Though he lived a happy life in Madrid, he had a difficult task; for as we have seen, France was unpopular with the Spanish people, and there were also such Spanish ministers as Arriaga and Squillace who disliked France. Ossun was, however, a hispanophile and known to be such. But a few years later the enlightened Spanish minister Floridablanca would say to the then French ambassador, "It seems that you look on the king of Spain as a kind of viceroy or provincial governor."

Beaumarchais left no account of his journey from Madrid to the court at Aranjuez, but we can imagine him leaving the capital by the traditional route over the narrow river Manzanares, by the new Puente de Toledo, in the middle of which there were parapets where San Isidro, the patron saint of Madrid, and his wife, Santa María de la Cabeza, were commemorated. These simple souls were the only husband and wife in the long history of the church both to be canonised.

Ossun lived in Aranjuez in one of the few houses in the village, some distance from the royal residence. He had received letters on Beaumarchais's behalf from the princesses. But he said to him, "The first proof of my friendship, sir, is to warn you that your journey to Spain is utterly useless in respect of avenging your sister; the man who has insulted her twice . . . would never have declared himself guilty if he had not been powerfully backed. What is your plan? Do you hope to make him marry your sister?"

"No, monsieur," returned Beaumarchais, "I do not want that, but I do want to dishonour him."

He then recounted his conversation with Clavijo, which the ambassador accepted as true when he read the declaration which Beaumarchais had persuaded Clavijo to sign. "*Eh bien, monsieur,*" said the ambassador in consequence,

I change my mind this instant. Anyone who can advance his affairs so well in two hours is certain to conclude them happily. Ambition took Clavijo away from Mademoiselle your sister, and ambition, terror, or love is taking him back to her. But with whatever title he returns, it must be right to do everything with the least *éclat*. I cannot disguise from you that this man is someone who will go far. And in consequence, he is a very good match. In your place, I would conquer your sister's reluctance and, profiting from the repentance of Clavijo, I would try and ensure that they are married immediately.

Beaumarchais asked: "How so, with a coward?"

"He will not be a coward if he returns in good faith. But that point agreed, he is only a repentant lover. For the rest, here is my advice. I invite you to follow it—and I admit that as well I find myself admiring you now for reasons which I cannot quite explain to you."

When Beaumarchais was back in Madrid, to his amazement he found that Clavijo had changed his mind yet again. He had first visited the Carons' house in the Calle de la Montera, with some friends, to throw himself at the feet of the sisters. But Lisette had kept to her room. Clavijo daily thereafter went to see Beaumarchais. He dined frequently with the Carons, and we must imagine him complimenting his hosts on the French innovations in the cooking; for the old Spanish *puchero* or *olla podrida,* the typical national dish, was giving way in those days of "the Family Compact" to all kinds of new French recipes such as the "fricandó" (from the French *fricandeau,* a veal stew) or a "fricasé" (from *fricassée*).

A week later, on May 25, Clavijo abandoned the house of Antonio de Portugués for a lodging in what Beaumarchais called the "quartier des Invalides." Presumably that was near the vast barracks of the Conde-Duque, with its three great patios, in the west of the capital. He explained to Beaumarchais that he had done this because his friend Portugués criticised the idea of his marriage.

Clavijo then wrote another contradictory letter to Beaumarchais on May 26:

I have explained firmly how I hope to make up for the chagrins which I have involuntarily caused Mademoiselle Caron; I offer again to marry her if the misunderstandings which have passed between us have not carried me too far from you. My proposals are sincere. My conduct and my actions are intended only to reconquer her heart. My happiness depends on the success of my efforts. I take the liberty of recognising that you have played an essential part in this happy reconciliation. I know that a gallant man does himself honour if he humiliates himself before a lady whom he has offended; and that perhaps also a man abases himself if he makes excuses before another man in respect of his mistakes in the eyes of someone of another sex. It is then in recognition of that that I act in this matter. . . . If it were possible for me to leave Madrid without an express order of my chief [Grimaldi], I would leave immediately for Aranjuez to ask for his approval; but I still expect from your friendship that you will yourself take the trouble to reflect the legitimate and honest views of mademoiselle your sister.

When Beaumarchais read this letter aloud to his sisters, Lisette burst into tears and Beaumarchais said: "Ah well, ah well, my child, you love him still and you are deeply ashamed of it, isn't that so? ... But all the same you are an excellent girl, and when your anger reaches its conclusion, let that time be put out by the tears of your pardon! They are certainly sweet to see after those of anger. He is a monster ... like most men! But, dear child, I agree with the Marquis de Ossun when he advises you to pardon him."

Beaumarchais wrote later: "My teasing made her smile in the midst of her tears; and I took the fact of this charming conflict between us as a tacit agreement with the view of Monsieur the ambassador." What in truth Lisette felt at this moment is hard to imagine. Did she really want Clavijo as her husband, or did she only want him humiliated? Beaumarchais sought out Clavijo, who again agreed to be received back into the Caron family and signed a letter to that effect before various friends of the two sisters, such as Señor Laugier, secretary of the embassy of Poland; Gazán, the consul of Spain at Bayonne; Devignes, a canon of Perpignan; Durocher, surgeon of the queen mother Elizabeth Farnese; the French merchants in Spain, the friends of Caron, Durand and Périer; Fermín de Salcedo, accountant of the king; the abbé Beliardi, a nominee of Choiseul who was the French commercial attaché; and Boca, an officer of the Walloon guard, as well as some others.

The letter read: "We the undersigned, José Clavijo and Marie-Louise Caron, by the present declaration renew the promises to be no longer separate beings; and we engage ourselves to sanctify these promises which we have made thousands of times by the sacrament of marriage as soon as possible. Marie-Louise and José."

FIVE

The Conquest of Clavijo

Clavijo's joint declaration with Lisette seemed an explicit enough undertaking. Everyone in the Carons' circle rejoiced again and passed the evening with the fiancé and with Beaumarchais. Then Beaumarchais left once more for Aranjuez, at eleven at night, because, he thought, "in a country as hot as Spain the night is the best time to travel." It was, after all, already summer. Next morning in Aranjuez, he told Ambassador Ossun of what had transpired. He also called on the foreign minister, Grimaldi, who had influenced the king to create in Aranjuez a model village with a double row of trees down the main avenue, following the plan of a similar Dutch village—he had previously been minister in The Hague. Grimaldi, said Beaumarchais, "received me with kindness, read the letter from Clavijo [as Clavijo's chief], gave his consent to the marriage, and sent every kind of good wish to my sister; remarking that Clavijo could have spared me the journey which I had made. I tried to recall all the eagerness which I had myself shown in coming to see him, before the moment when I asked him to honour me with being received to talk of the other important subjects on my mind." Those matters were, of course, Pâris-Duverney's ambitious commercial ideas for the pursuit of a French contract for the slave trade, of the monopoly of trade in Louisiana, of the licence to sell goods to the Spanish army, and of the colonisation of the Sierra Morena.

On his return to Madrid, thinking that at least one part of his work in Madrid was done, Beaumarchais found a new aggressive letter from Clavijo enclosing another written by d'Aubarède when he left Clavijo the first time: "Here, sir, is the unworthy document which has been distributed to the public, both at court and in the city. My honour is outraged in a most deadly manner and I dare not even put my head outdoors while such base ideas of my character and my honour are being entertained. I pray you, sir, to look at the declaration which I have myself signed and to give me copies of it. Waiting for the world to be disabused of its illusions, it is not convenient that we should meet for several days. Imagine, monsieur, in what desolation an outrage like this leaves me."

Clavijo attached to this letter what Beaumarchais called "an abominable, false, and monstrous declaration" in his own hand.

Beaumarchais went immediately to Clavijo to reproach him. He found him in bed. Beaumarchais promised him that once everything was settled, he would go about Madrid with him as if he were his brother. They then began making all the arrangements for Lisette's marriage. Even the Nuncio was apprised.

Beaumarchais also made a remarkable proposal to Clavijo: "My dear friend, the state of our relationship now allows me to take certain liberties with you; if you are not feeling flush with money, you would do well to accept this purse into which I have put gold pieces worth 9,000 livres in French money, from which you could pay 25 quadruples to my sister for fripperies; and here are jewels and lace from France; if you want to make her a present, she would receive them from your hand even more enthusiastically than from mine."

Clavijo accepted the jewels and the lace but refused the money.

Next day the mestizo valet whom Beaumarchais had hired in Bayonne robbed him of all that was left in cash, his gold and silver currency, his purse, the silver in his dressing case, a box of lace clothes, all his silk stockings, and some shirts, worth together about fifteen thousand francs. The thief was never seen again. Beaumarchais immediately went to complain to Colonel Robiou, the commandant of Madrid, who received him with a surprisingly icy air, even though he was an old acquaintance, having consulted Caron's father in the 1740s about his system for the control of rivers. Beaumarchais later pointed out that if Clavijo had only accepted his offer, his losses would have been minimized. Clavijo said that the valet would certainly not only have set off for Cádiz but would probably already be leaving for the Indies on a ship in the official treasure fleet. Beaumarchais told his ambassador about the theft but did not concern himself more about the matter. He had enough letters of credit to make up for the loss. Everything otherwise seemed in good shape for the wedding.

Early in June, Beaumarchais received a letter from his father, who wrote, "How delighted I feel, my dear Beaumarchais, at the pleasure of being the father of a son whose actions crown so gloriously the end of my career. . . . Oh my dear friend what a beautiful wedding present is the declaration of Clavijo."

But by the time this letter reached him, Beaumarchais had heard, to his surprise, that Clavijo had again changed his address. He had left "les Invalides." Acting as a good policeman, Beaumarchais had a search made of all the *hotels garnis* of Madrid, from the best hotel, the Cruz de Malta in the Calle del Caballero de Gracia, downwards. He found him in lodgings in the Red de San Luis—not at all far from where the Caron sisters lived in the Calle de la Montera. Beaumarchais asked why he had not taken an apartment in the building of his sister. Clavijo answered a little illogically that he could not do that because he had begun to take medicine for a sudden fever and could not go out.

Beaumarchais soon learned that in Spain all legal responsibilities were nullified if it turned out that someone had been taking medicine. Suspicion returned. Lisette, of course, trembled anew. So Beaumarchais went to seek the approval of the apostolic notary for the wedding. But that official made an astonishing statement that the previous day he had received a formal document opposing the marriage of Clavijo: a chambermaid who had once worked for Antonio de Portugués, Clavijo's friend, said that she had had a promise of marriage from Clavijo dated 1755.

Beaumarchais went to protest to Clavijo:

This marriage promise is something which you made up yesterday. You are such an abominable man that I would not have my sister marry you for all the treasure of the Indies. This evening I leave again for Aranjuez. I shall inform Monsieur Grimaldi of your infamy; and, far from opposing the marriage of my sister as if I were a duenna, I shall demand as my unique vengeance that you marry her on the spot. I shall act as her father, I will pay her dowry, and will make all my services available to her until she takes you to the altar. Thus, caught in your own trap, you will be dishonoured and I shall be avenged.

Clavijo replied:

Suspend your resentments and your journey until tomorrow. I had no part in this black blot. It is true that I was long ago engaged to the duenna of the señor de Portugués, who was pretty but with whom I have had nothing to do since our rupture years ago. It is the enemies of Doña María who have inspired this lady. But believe me the way out of this is a matter of a few pistoles d'or. I will invite you this evening to talk to a famous lawyer who will accompany you to Aranjuez and we shall discuss, before you leave, some way of dealing with this new obstacle which is a good deal less important than your imagination makes you think. Put me at the feet of Doña María, your sister, whom I propose to love all her life. And don't fail to be here at eight sharp this evening.

Beaumarchais confessed to himself that his heart was bitter, his mind indecisive. Had he been played with by a clown? But if so, what was Clavijo's real aim? Not being able to guess the answer, Beaumarchais suspended judgement.

About eight in the evening, all the same, Beaumarchais returned once more to go and see this utterly unpredictable Clavijo, accompanied by his French friends the bankers Périer and Durand. When they arrived at the lodgings in the Red de San Luis, the housekeeper said, "Señor Clavijo left an hour ago and I have no idea where he has gone." Beaumarchais went to the room where his supposed brother-in-law-to-be had been living. None of his effects were there. Returning home to the Carons', he arranged for six men to search the entire capital in the hope of finding the traitor, at whatever cost. The city was not then large: about 140,000 people. The searchers found nothing. Beaumarchais had run out of ideas when an urgent letter came from Ossun, the French ambassador, still in Aranjuez.

The ambassador wrote that Colonel de Robiou, the military commandant of Madrid, whom Beaumarchais had already rather unhappily encountered, has just called on me to inform me that Monsieur Clavijo had returned to a lodging in the Invalides and has declared that he is taking asylum because, according to him, a few days ago in his own house, you forced him, a pistol at his head, to sign a document by which he undertook to marry Mademoiselle your sister. However honest and correct your conduct in this affair has been, the present turn of events could be most disagreeable and troublesome for you. Thus I advise you to remain entirely calm in everything you say, in your writings and in your actions until I see you, either here, if you come back quickly, or in Madrid, where I return on the 12th.

This was a thunderbolt. What, the francophile man of letters, who for two weeks had been pressing Beaumarchais in his arms, was now threatening him? This "monster" who, in numerous letters, had asked publicly for the hand of Lisette, who had dined with her and Beaumarchais at least ten times in her house, was making a criminal charge which included an accusation that Beaumarchais had threatened him!

An officer of the Walloon guards (two-thirds of the guards of the king were Walloons, much as the king of France and the pope had their Swiss guards) was then announced and said: "Monsieur de Beaumarchais, you don't have a moment to lose; you should know that tomorrow morning you will be arrested in your bed. The order has been given; I have come to warn you. The man Clavijo may be a monster, but he has stirred up official feeling against you and after many promises has become your public accuser. Fly, fly this second or be prepared for a dungeon where you will have neither protection nor defence."

"Me fly! To save my skin!" thought Beaumarchais. "Better die!" He then said to his friends in the Carons' house, "Don't talk to me any more, only arrange that tomorrow morning at five o'clock I have a coach with six mules ready for me and let me rest a little before I leave for Aranjuez."

Beaumarchais rested two hours in an armchair, then went to the room which he had been using as his office, where he wrote till five in the morning, giving a detailed account of everything he had done in Madrid. The carriage, probably a *calesa*, a small two-wheeled carriage drawn by mules, rather like a French cabriolet, came at five, and he then left alone for Aranjuez for the third time. The journey of thirty miles would take ten hours.

The ambassador was still, in the evening of the next day, at the royal palace when Beaumarchais arrived at his house. So he could see him only at 11 P.M., when he returned home from his evening activities. "You have done well to come here to me immediately," Ossun said. "I was not at all happy about you. During the last fifteen days, your man [Clavijo] has captured all the paths which lead to the palace. Without me you would be lost; perhaps anyway you will be arrested and taken to the criminal court called the Presidio. I have been talking to Monsieur de Grimaldi," he went on. "I spoke of the good conduct of Monsieur de Beaumarchais in this whole affair as if it were my own. I explained, 'He is a man of honour who has only done what you and I would do if we were in his place. I have followed his actions since his arrival. Do please withdraw the order to arrest him. It derives from the atrocious behaviour of his adversary.'"

"I believe you," Grimaldi had told the ambassador, "but I am able to suspend things only for a moment. Everyone is becoming armed against him. Tell him to leave immediately for France. We can shut our eyes to his flight." Grimaldi loved France, but, as we have seen, his was not a strong personality, and his position was frequently undermined by his own colleague, Squillace.

"So, Monsieur, you must leave," the ambassador said to Beaumarchais. "There is no time to lose. We shall send your effects to Paris after you. You have six mules at your disposal. At all costs, tomorrow morning, take the road to France. I cannot help you, with the general mood of the country against you, in the face of such precise orders. And I should be desolated if some unhappiness were to befall you in this country. Leave!"

Beaumarchais was tempted to weep. From time to time, he admitted, large tears fell from his eyes. He seemed suddenly stupid, silent. The ambassador was full of kindness, agreeing that, of course, he was in the right, but saying that he had to be realistic, and to flee in order to escape what would otherwise be certain unhappiness.

"And what would I be being punished for, Monsieur," asked Beaumarchais, "since even you accept that I am right on all the points at issue? Could the king of Spain seriously arrest an innocent and gravely injured man? How is it possible that someone such as he who has the power to do everything prefers an evil course when he knows what is good?"

"Well, Monsieur, the order of the king has to be carried out, and evil is done when that does not happen. Kings are just. But people intrigue around them without their knowing it. And malign interests and resentments which one does not dare to admit are often the source of all the evil which is done. Once arrested, there is no one here who has taken an interest in you who will not think that, because you are being punished, you must have done something wrong; and the pressure of other events will soon make them forget what happened to you; for the fecklessness of public opinion is always one of the strongest supports of injustice. So, leave, I say to you, leave."

"But do you personally want me to leave?"

"Your brain troubles you excessively. Avoid a certain evil and think that perhaps you will only twice in your life have the occasion for reflections so sad for humanity; you will perhaps never again be unworthily insulted by a man more powerful than you are; you will perhaps never again run the risk of being imprisoned for having taken a stand which was prudent, firm, and reasonable, against a madman."

"But, Monsieur, what will be the attitude of my friends? What will be the reaction of my august protectresses the French princesses, who, having seen me constantly teased around them [in Paris], have been able to believe at least that I did not merit the evil which used sometimes to be said of me? They would believe that my honesty was only a mask which fell away at the first chance that I found to do evil with impunity."

"Don't worry, Monsieur, I will write to France and my word will be accepted."

"And my sister, my unhappy sister who is no more guilty than I am?"

"Think of yourself, we shall look after the others."

"Ah, God, God, so this will be the fruit of my journey to Spain!"

But "leave" was the word which Monsieur de Ossun could not stop saying. He offered Beaumarchais money if he needed it.

"Monsieur, I have enough; I have a thousand louis in my purse and two hundred thousand louis in my wallet, to enable me to continue to pursue this brutal outrage."

"No, Monsieur, I cannot agree to it. You were highly recommended to me. Leave, I beg you, I advise you urgently and I would go further still if it were necessary."

"I do not understand you any more, monsieur, forgive me, I cannot understand."

Beaumarchais left the room furious and, having arranged no lodging, passed the night under Philip II's noble trees in the solemn avenues of the park of Aranjuez. He was untroubled by the wild boar and deer which roamed. But it was for him all the same a night of extraordinary agitation. He had not, after all, come to Spain only to save his sister from Clavijo. The whole series of other opportunities as proposed by Pâris-Duverney had still to be discussed.

Next morning, confirmed in his determination, resolved to die or be avenged, Beaumarchais went to the levée in the house of the foreign minister Grimaldi. This was a short distance from the salon where the king himself was receiving visitors. One can easily imagine the courtiers and would-be courtiers approaching the house of the foreign minister in their frills and ruffles, picking their way across the dust of the courtyard, after an uncomfortable night in one of the cheap lodging places where they might have been sleeping.

Beaumarchais was waiting in an anteroom for his turn with Grimaldi when he heard the name "Monsieur Wall" called out several times. Richard Wall was the Irish general who had been the immediate predecessor of Grimaldi as foreign minister—and the benefactor of Clavijo. It had been said that he had resigned his ministry only because he wanted to have a brief interval between his work and his death. He was temporarily living in the house of Grimaldi, with whom he was on good terms, an unusual thing in respect of a relation between two ministers.

Wall had retired pretending that his sight was bad, wore a shade over his eyes, and used an ointment to secure relief from their temporary inflammation. He planned to live most of the year in his house outside Granada (the same which the Duke of Wellington would later be given after the wars against Napoleon). His plan was to attend the court at Aranjuez for a month, then return to the city of Granada, where he had another house.

Beaumarchais had himself announced to Wall as a foreigner

who had an important matter to communicate to him. There was no one else waiting for him: a retired minister was rarely a useful ally in the battle for place.

"The foreigner" was immediately ushered in.

"Monsieur," Beaumarchais said to him, "I have no other call to gain your assistance than that of being an outraged Frenchman. You were yourself born in France, where you have served." That was not quite so; Wall had been born in the depths of old Ireland at Coolnamuck, Waterford. But he had served in Paris. "Since then, you have been in that country at every level of military and political activity. But all these titles give me less confidence to have recourse to you than the true grandeur with which you have handed back voluntarily to the king the valuable ministry of the Indies when any other man might have laid his hands on millions. [This was an allusion to Wall's rearrangement of the portfolio concerned with the empire from the Foreign Ministry to the Ministry of Marine.] With the esteem of the nation you have remained the friend of the king; you have a name which honours you without any qualification. Very well, Monsieur, there remains one fine thing to do; it is worthy of you; and it is a Frenchman in despair who counts on the help of a man as virtuous as you are."

"You are from France, Monsieur," Wall replied in French. "That is a good recommendation for me. I have always loved France and I would like to be able to compensate for all the good treatment which I have received there. But you tremble, your soul is out of control; sit down and tell me your troubles. They must be frightful if they are equal to the distress in which I see you." In fact, Wall had the reputation when a minister of being a great friend of England and had opposed the "Family Pact."

Beaumarchais asked Wall permission to read out his journal of events in Madrid since his arrival. The astonished ex-minister agreed and locked his door. Beaumarchais began to read. Wall calmed him from time to time, asking him to read more slowly so that he could understand better, but assuring him that he took a great interest in the story. Beaumarchais told him everything, and read aloud to him all the letters which he had received from Clavijo or had written to him. When he told him of the new criminal case against him, how that had been suspended only by the intervention of Ossun and Grimaldi, and that only for a time, Wall became converted into the latest of those enchanted by Beaumarchais's charm, energy, impertinence, and daring. He cried out, rose from his chair and, embracing Beaumarchais tenderly, said,

> Without doubt, the king will do you justice, and you have reason to count on him. Your ambassador, despite his kindness to you, is obliged to consult here the delicacy of his status; but I, I am going to serve your vengeance with all my influence. No, Monsieur, it must not be said that a brave Frenchman has left his country, his protectors, his affairs, his pleasures, and that he has travelled four hundred leagues to help an honest and unhappy sister and that, in running away from this country, he carries back, in his

heart, an abominable idea of the generous Spanish nation as a place where foreigners do not receive justice. I will act as a father to you on this occasion just as you have acted similarly for your sister.

Wall continued,

It was I who recommended this Clavijo to the king. I am guilty of that crime; ah, ye gods, how people in power are so unfortunate as to be unable to examine with adequate care the men whom they employ and with whom they surround themselves, without knowing anything of the scoundrels whose infamies are too often attributed to them themselves. This, Monsieur, is more important to me than Clavijo, who, beginning to publish a kind of newsletter or gazette, was able one day to obtain one of the best jobs under the Crown; and yet it was I who made a present to the king of his services. One can excuse a minister for being deceived in the choice of an unworthy subject; but, as soon as he sees him marked by the seal of public reprobation, he owes it to himself to chase him away on the instant. I am going to give an example to all ministers who follow me.

Wall rang. He ordered horses, took Beaumarchais to the main entrance of the palace, and went in to see the king, to whom he presented himself as having been responsible for the crimes of Clavijo. He had pressed the suit of that writer and now he was pressing even harder to secure his fall. Grimaldi also came in, and the two ministers insisted that Beaumarchais go in to see the king himself. Beaumarchais bowed low. "Read out your memoir," Monsieur Wall said with warmth. "There could be no honest soul who would not be touched by it as I was."

Beaumarchais recalled that he had "his heart in his mouth," he felt it beat with an extraordinary force in his breast, and, delivering himself up to what might be called the eloquence of the moment, he came back to the text with energy and rapidity and read to King Charles everything which he had just read to Wall.

Then the king, now sufficiently well informed, ordered that Clavijo be dismissed from his appointment as archivist of the Crown. He would be asked to leave his offices immediately. Charles III also sent a message to Ambassador Ossun, with whom Beaumarchais was to dine that night, to give instructions to send him a copy of the journal which had been read to him with such advantage. Ossun asked some secretaries to set about copying this as soon as they could. It was personally carried by Ossun to the king.

Beaumarchais returned from Aranjuez to Madrid, where all the French in town pressed forward to renew their old friendship to his sister. The news of Clavijo's loss of employment was known immediately. Clavijo, certain of being arrested, fled to the Capuchin monastery in the Calle Atocha, from which he wrote a long and eloquent letter to Beaumarchais begging for sympathy. He could certainly have expected that, because Beaumarchais—at least according to himself—never hated anyone for long. But very conveniently he did not mention the criminal case which he had mounted against Beaumarchais. He gave no explanation, and made no apology, for his extraordinary conduct.

With his usual astonishing good nature, Beaumarchais later requested Grimaldi to pardon Clavijo. After all, as has been pointed out earlier, the Francophile Clavijo was just the man who, all things being equal, would have enchanted the French. He was, in a sense, a self-appointed French agent. But Grimaldi refused with such a furious indignation that Beaumarchais did not dare to insist. He had not secured his sister's marriage to Clavijo. But he had succeeded in having Clavijo punished for his bad conduct, and the event seemed a triumph for Beaumarchais, who thought that the name for persistence which he had gained in these weeks would assist him in his numerous other projects. A few months later, he wrote to his future brother-in-law Miron in Paris that he had persuaded Lisette to remain a spinster.

The experience of these conversations also naturally convinced Beaumarchais of the wisdom of the king, whom he never ceased to praise for all kinds of actions not directly related to himself.

The real explanation of Clavijo's conduct is hidden from us. He seems to be an interesting example of a man in love with France, but not really with Lisette. Perhaps something in his soul told him that, though he might be a good fiancé, he would never be a good husband.

SIX

The Pursuit of Profit

As we know, Beaumarchais had many reasons to be in Madrid other than the help which he wanted to offer his sister. All the same, it was now midsummer, and he must have been caught up by the celebrations which swept through Spain commemorating Corpus Christi, with processions of *cabezudos* (men disguised with large heads who put children to flight), giants of both sexes who danced in honour of the four continents, and a *tarasca* (dragon). The processions would have astonished Beaumarchais, since nothing like them were then to be seen in France. But such characters continue to appear in Spanish fiestas even in the twenty-first century, to the delight of many. At that time, Madrid was almost as dominated by such ceremonies as was Andalusia, whereas today such manifestations in the capital are feeble; and Corpus Christi was then almost as much celebrated as was Easter, whereas today even in Andalusia that festival makes only a modest showing. But in the eighteenth century, the long marches of paupers, orphans, pious brotherhoods, magistrates, representatives of the religious orders, followed by the ecclesiastical council, the bishop, and even the councils of the realm, with the royal Walloon guards bringing up the rear (the guards which Beaumarchais came to know), seemed a reminder of the *engrenage* of church and state. Perhaps it was now, watching the crowds waiting for the arrival of the floats on which the figures of Christs and Virgins were carried, that Beaumarchais made his judgement about the Spaniards: "They are generally good, sober and, above all, very patient."

Beaumarchais, continuing to stay with his sisters in the Calle de la Montera, turned his attention now to the serious matters which Pâris-Duverney had wanted him to pursue and which Maurice Lever thought constituted the true explanation for Beaumarchais's journey. The idea that he might become the commissary of the Spanish armed forces was an intoxicating one for Pâris-Duverney. He knew from experience how that type of contract could lead to vast profits. He must have known that, for example, in the late war the commissary of the British fleet which captured Havana, John Kennion of Rochdale and Jamaica, had made a fortune by introducing English goods and English slaves into the conquered city.

But Beaumarchais found great difficulty in making any headway in respect of any of his projects. The essential reason was the

Portrait of Beaumarchais by Jean-Marc Nattier.
Bibliothèque de la Comédie Française, Paris

King Charles III of Spain signs a document allowing trade with the New World.
P. P. Montaña. Delegación del Gobierno en Cataluña, Barcelona

King Louis XV of France surrounded by his daughters (clockwise from upper right)
Madame Sophie, Madame Marie Adélaïde, Madame Victoire, and Madame Louise.
Portraits by F. H. Drouais (Louis) and Jean-Marc Nattier. Musée de Versailles

Richard Wall, the Irish-born secretary of state in Spain who saved Beaumarchais.
Painter unknown. Museo Naval, Madrid

Jerónimo Grimaldi, the Genoese foreign minister of Spain who loved France.
Portrait by Antonio de Marón. Colección Carderera, Biblioteca Nacional, Madrid

Joseph Pâris-Duverney, the financier who treated Beaumarchais as the son he never had. Engraving by Dujardin, from a portrait by L. M. Vanloo

The Marqués de Croix, whose wife was probably Beaumarchais's mistress in Madrid. From an anonymous print

The Calle de Platerías, in Madrid, adorned to welcome the arrival of
King Charles III. From a painting by Lorenzo de Quirós in the Museo Municipal,
Madrid. Inv. 3073. Depósito de la Real Academia de Bellas Artes de San Fernando

Luis Paret y Alcázar, *Charles III dining before his court*. Museo del Prado, Madrid

A *seguidilla*. Engraving by Marcos Téllez. Museo Municipal, Madrid

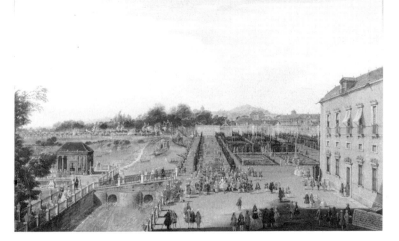

Francesco Battaglioli, King Ferdinand VI and Queen Barbara of Braganza with their guests in the gardens of the palace of Aranjuez. Museo del Prado, Madrid

A scene from the *sainete* "Manolo" by Ramón de la Cruz. Beaumarchais loved these playlets when in Madrid. From an anonymous print. Museo Municipal, Madrid

The Paseo del Prado in Madrid, c. 1760. In *The Barber of Seville*,
the Count of Almaviva first saw Rosine here.
Tapestry after a painting by Ramón Bayeu. Patrimonio Nacional, Madrid

Jacopo Amigoni, *Fiesta galante en un jardín:* a garden party in Madrid.
Could the Marquesa de Croix be there in white? Museo del Prado, Madrid

Miguel Ángel Houasse, *Una Velada Musical:* a musical party in Madrid. Could it be the Countess Buturlin at the harpsichord? Patrimonio Nacional, Madrid

Luis Paret y Alcázar, a party in the botanical gardens, Madrid. Museo de Lázaro Galdiano, Madrid

Luis Meléndez, still life of a Spanish picnic. Museo del Prado, Madrid

Spanish popular dislike of France. In those days any dandified courtier in Madrid might be seized by the townspeople and asked to pronounce the word *ajo* (garlic) or *cebolla* (onion). If he could not, he ran the risk of being beaten up for the crime "of being French." Partly this was because common people resented the penetration of French customs among the upper class or would-be upper class. Frenchmen were popularly called *gabachos* (literally people of the Pyrenees). But that did not prevent the introduction of French dress into the army, nor the coming of the powdered wig (*peluquines*) as a substitute for hair gathered into a silk net. Tight-fitting waistcoats and breeches in the French style were to be seen everywhere by 1760, along with other marks of modernity such as the three-cornered "French hat." But profound hostility to France continued throughout the eighteenth century, and it goes a long way to explain the remarkable violence of the Spanish resistance to the French invasion by Napoleon, and indeed the right-wing hostility to liberalism in the nineteenth century, as well as the twentieth. The "fanatical fury and feverish patriotism" of Spain in the Napoleonic wars "disconcerted all the statesmen of Europe," Albert Sorel commented in his great book *Europe and the French Revolution*, recalling the comment of a Spanish peasant that "his father would have risen from his tomb if he had seen a chance of a war with the French."

At one level, the Spaniards cherished their family pact with France, but in the 1760s there was rivalry between the two senior ministers responsible for the matter: Squillace, the Neapolitan formally responsible for war and the treasury, was jealous of his

Genoese colleague Grimaldi. Anything which Grimaldi liked, such as friendship with France, was automatically opposed by Squillace. Beaumarchais had, as we have seen, a friendship with the first, none with the latter. Ambassadors who went first to Grimaldi were sidelined by Squillace.

The young prince of Asturias, the future Charles IV, though he seemed still a person of little consequence, was also opposed to the French connection, apparently because of having been educated by two German Jesuits chosen by his late mother Queen María-Amalia.

Beaumarchais came to know well several leaders of the Spanish political system, but decisions were often made at a lower level and he had little patience and no gift for dealing effectively with minor officials. He later complained to his father, "This country is a hydra of delay and commonplace obstacles."

All the same, Beaumarchais's "incurable optimism" caused him to suppose that all would prosper in his different projects. He had the cynicism of intelligent youth, as his plays show. But at the same time he had the optimism of innocence. The first matter which he tried to settle was Pâris-Duverney's plan for a contract to provide the Spanish army with its rations. He devoted much attention to this in the summer of 1764 and was still working on it in the winter, by which time he had expected to be back in Paris. Thus he wrote to his father on December 3, 1764, that the court had returned to Madrid the previous day from the Escorial.

All the ministers are here. I shall fight vigorously to gain a definite decision about the undertaking, which has only a single point of difficulty. This is that it must do nothing between the ministers and private people which does not provide the king with a guarantee of control. The king and the minister Squillace appear happy with my work and my offers. The prices would be arranged so advantageously for me that the matter is something almost limitless in its consequences. I have pointed out to the minister that I have not asked for any advance, which is the only thing for which a guarantee might be necessary. I have, however, divided my argument into two sections: first, if His Majesty would in fact like to advance me (which is normal in any governmental undertaking of this size) six months' worth of payments for provisions, which I would calculate would be seven million livres, I would give him a Spanish guarantee covering exactly what is paid to me. . . . And, if His Majesty advances me nothing, I hope that he will find it reasonable if I do not spend anything out of my possible profit to pay for a guarantee. I cannot hide the fact that Lumbreras, the richest businessman in Madrid, is running after me. . . . But I am well up in the matter.

He added, with optimism as usual playing a part: "While my bad luck has meant that I have lost two thousand *écus* of income on rations from France which have been allowed to rot entirely in order to ruin me, the king of Spain and the minister look on me as being the animator of those things in Spain as Pâris-Duverney is in France." This was a real statement of *folie de petit grandeur*.

Beaumarchais went on to his father: "That is why I have made my submission. One could add to that the general provisioning of grain from Spain for the nourishment of the people . . . also the manufacture of gunpowder and saltpetre in such a way that I could find myself at the head responsible for the supply of both food and munitions. Please keep all this a secret."

In the afternoon of the same day, Beaumarchais wrote to his father again, more cautiously

I am both a little farther advanced than I was this morning and also a little less far. Caution persists, and it is all a matter of calculation. I am having to draw up my conditions in the clearest possible manner. During this time, I am working to get rid of the guarantee. The affair of the food supplies is already arranged at 16 *maravedís* per ration of bread, and 16 *reales* the *fanega* or *quintal* of barley. . . . The entrepreneur who had the same contract previously had the same arrangement that I have at 14 *maravedís* and 14 *reales,* and the matter turned out well for him. Grain is admittedly expensive so I am working at the highest price and can expect little gain this year. . . . I am at the moment in a state of all or nothing.

But none of these efforts led to anything positive. The Neapolitan minister, Squillace, was determined to avoid anything which might seem like a French solution to any of Spain's problems, especially so where it affected anything so important as the provisioning of the army.

As for Pâris-Duverney's schemes for the colonisation of unpopulated areas, the idea for the settlement of the Sierra Morena may have attracted Beaumarchais for literary reasons. He had no doubt read *Don Quixote*, perhaps in the new edition published in Lyon in 1738. He would have found many allusions there to those beautiful, dangerous, and bandit-haunted mountains. For example: in chapter 23 of the first part we read, "Don Quixote leaped on his horse without replying a word. Sancho guided him on his mule. They both entered into that part of the Sierra Morena that was near unto them. Sancho had a secret design to cross over it all and come out at Viso or Almodóvar del Campo and, in the meantime, to hide among those craggy and intricate rocks so that they might not be found by the Holy Brotherhood [the equivalent of the police] if it should pursue them."

German states had used the expedient of colonisation in deserted areas of their country for a century, and Pâris-Duverney thought that the same could be done in Spain. He knew that such settlements might be founded in lonely regions along the main road from Madrid to Seville, and in the Sierra Morena itself. Land, houses, and agricultural tools, as well as livestock, would be given to the colonists by the Crown, which would in return receive rent in kind. To avoid the growth of large estates (*latifundia*), which were seen by enlightened reformers as the curse of Spanish agriculture, the new owners would be prohibited from selling, mortgaging, dividing, or expanding their properties. Animals could be grazed on common lands, while certain other lands would be tilled in common to pay for the expenses of the villages. All monastic or conventual institutions were to be excluded, and the famous Mesta, the organisation which managed the annual movements of the sheep of Spain from one pasture to another in summer and winter, would not be permitted entry.

On September 20, 1764, Beaumarchais wrote to his friend and ally the banker Jean Durand, Lisette's sometime fiancé, asking him to discover all he could about that part of Spain: what was the average temperature in those mountains? Was there a good supply of water? Was the land which was being considered closer to El Viso, the last town of the Mancha, or to Bailén, the first town of Andalusia? Or did it perhaps lie in the large space thirty miles broad between those places? Were there rivers or streams which were, or could be made, navigable? What was the quality of the soil? Were the mountains so high as to make travel difficult? Was there snow in winter, rain in summer? How far was the region from Madrid? Did the land concerned march with the property of the Duke of Medina Sidonia? Would it be necessary to make bricks to build the planned village? What were the natural products?

But here again, as in relation to the question of the provisioning of the army, Beaumarchais came up against patriotic opposition.

The consequence was that no decision was for the moment made on the matter and, two years later, in 1767, the government decided to allocate the plan for the colonisation of the Sierra Morena to a Bavarian soldier, Johann Gaspar Thürriegel, who, like Beaumarchais, came to Spain to seek his fortune. He was supported by the enlightened intendant, an administrator introduced by the Bourbons in imitation of a similar French office, Pablo de Olavide, who knew that the prospects of the best of schemes could be ruined if it turned out that Frenchmen would profit from it. Germans were different. So one thousand families eventually came from Switzerland and many others came from Germany. Casanova became interested and tried to encourage the colonists to marry Spaniards. The modern town of Carolina is a surviving memory of the policy.

Beaumarchais wrote in respect of this: "The prejudice against the customs of foreigners is carried to excess in this country by the populace, and many distinguished people in this respect are in agreement. We are the least spared. But I accept that the sharp tone of French people who come here contributes to maintain this kind of hatred; it is a bitterness which is repaid in mockery."

The next matter on Beaumarchais's agenda was the licence to trade slaves to the Spanish empire.

This was an immense undertaking. Though Spain had nearly as large an appetite for African slaves as the other European empires in the New World, her monarchs had allowed the African trade to remain largely with the Portuguese. There was no legal commerce of any kind of Spaniards with Guinea or elsewhere in

Africa, except for a small stretch of land facing the Canary Islands which eventually became Spanish Sahara. The Portuguese were accustomed to selling the slaves that they needed to the Spaniards in the New World. From the seventeenth century onwards, other countries benefited from these openings: merchants from Genoa, for example, then the Dutch West Indies Company, even though the Dutch were Protestant. Finally, in the early eighteenth century, after an astute expenditure of a million pesos, the French captured the contract (*asiento*). Profits were divided between the two Bourbon monarchs, one of France, one of Spain. Jean-Baptiste Ducasse, a French captain who had saved the important slave trading island of Gorée near the Sénégal river for the French Crown in the war of the Spanish succession and who afterwards became governor of the colony, richer every year, of Saint-Domingue, was also to have a share. This was not a popular concession. But it was a success. The French Guinea Company probably carried ten or twelve thousand slaves into the Spanish empire between 1702 and 1712.

In 1713 the Treaty of Utrecht gave the Protestant English the sought-after licence, alongside the right to sponsor a fair every year in two places in the empire (at Portobelo, on the Isthmus of Panama, and at Jalapa, outside Veracruz in New Spain, Mexico) to promote their goods. The French saw their failure to gain this licence as a serious setback. All the same, by the treaty they could only sit back and watch as the English government formed their South Sea Company to take advantage of this opportunity.

Later wars and other setbacks showed the South Sea Company

to be inadequate and incompetent, and, after some other experiments, the licence to carry slaves into the Spanish empire in 1764 again became available. In the meantime, with the Spanish-American demand greater every year, much illegal trading of slaves occurred, especially carried on by English captains. Captains from Liverpool, Bristol, and Newport, Rhode Island, were in particular busy carrying Africans to work in the new sugar industry of the beautiful Spanish island of Cuba.

The question of the morality of this traffic had already been posed by enlightened writers in France. But France's own Saint-Domingue, the richest colony in the world, was at that time the most voracious consumer of Africans, as Beaumarchais would have known from his enquiries into the extent of the fortune of his beautiful Creole friend Pauline Le Breton. The complaints of a few writers were not enough to prevent an increase every year of slaves imported into that island. All the same the wise Montesquieu, the witty Marivaux, the thoughtful Diderot, and other contributors to the latter's *Encyclopaedia* had all condemned slavery and mocked the slave trade. The great Voltaire, then seen as the father of all wisdom, had a somewhat ambiguous stand, it is true: though he had laughed at slavery on several occasions, he had nevertheless allowed René Montaudoin, the richest merchant of Nantes, to name one of his slaving vessels after him. He had also remarked, in his recent *Essai sur les moeurs:* "After all, the Africans sell their own people, we only buy them, so we must be superior."

It must seem odd that Beaumarchais, an enlightened rationalist, could involve himself in something at first sight so disgraceful as the trade in slaves. Had he not written a poem only a year before which took a critical stand on the matter? The verse ended

> *I know that the author of my life*
> *Created me free but, yet, I serve.*
> *Am I evil, impious, or just naïve*
> *When I sadly cry with verve:*
> *All is so bad in the universe.*

But soon after writing those lines, Beaumarchais met people from such ports as Nantes and La Rochelle who knew all about the slave trade to the Antilles and elsewhere in America from personal observation: people who did not talk sentimentally in the abstract but who argued that the conditions of life of Africans were so appalling in their own countries that Europeans did them a service if they offered them opportunities in the New World. Further, if the Africans sold their slaves to the French, say, they would encounter masters more humane than the Arabs who would probably buy them if Europeans did not. The French paid well for these slaves, even if usually in kind, and money in specie also passed from France to swell the budgets of, say, the kings of Dahomey or Congo. Pâris-Duverney never allowed morality to interfere with his commercial interests. Choiseul, Beaumarchais's chief political patron, thought that the slave trade was "the motor of all the others."

After the Peace of Paris of 1763, the first contract for trading slaves to be granted in the Spanish Empire was one by the new captain-general in Havana, the Conde de Ricla, to Martín José de Alegría of Cádiz, allowing him to import seven thousand slaves to Cuba. Alejandro O'Reilly, the general responsible for building new defences in the island, believed, as he said in April 1764 that "the prosperity of this island depends mainly on the import of African slaves." He added: "The king [too] will derive much more revenue from the import duties."

Seven thousand slaves was a large number for Cuba at that time, but much work was then being embarked upon on the defences of Havana to obstruct another invasion such as the English had so successfully mounted in 1762. In addition, the sugar planters of Cuba had realised, after the nine months of British occupation, that vast fortunes could be made by selling their product on the world market as well as to Spain.

Those considerations affected only Cuba. But at that time Mexico, northern South America (especially New Granada in modern Colombia), Argentina, and Peru also had an appetite for African slaves. Africans seemed so hardworking, so strong, so reliable, so good-natured in comparison with the local Indians. So a new large-scale asiento of the old kind was proposed.

The foremost candidate for this undertaking was a Basque merchant, Miguel de Uriarte, who lived in Cádiz in the south of Spain. Uriarte wanted a ten-year contract to sell slaves throughout Spanish America, at three hundred pesos a head. He urged that neither his goods nor his ships should be taxed, because, he thought, he would be providing an essential service. He would buy his slaves where he could, mostly in other ports of the Caribbean, and then take them for resale to a general Spanish imperial slave market in San Juan, Puerto Rico. Spanish merchants still did not expect then to go to Africa direct to obtain their slaves, though they soon would. At that time, they had neither the experience nor the legal basis for such a change in their commercial policies.

Uriarte did not have an easy task to convince the authorities in Madrid of his virtues. He had two serious competitors: a firm named Herrera, Silva, and Tamayo of Madrid, and Beaumarchais. The first's interest was fairly easily outmanoeuvred; but Beaumarchais's proposals were taken seriously in the knowledge that behind Beaumarchais was the vast wealth of Joseph Pâris-Duverney. The minister responsible for taking the decision on these matters was his acquaintance, Grimaldi, but the Council of the Indies, which had been since the sixteenth century the major committee dealing with imperial affairs, was really decisive in this matter. Beaumarchais could point out to that body the immense recent success of Nantes as an international trading port. After the French failure to win the asiento at the time of the Treaty of Utrecht, the French Crown had indeed opened up trade to the New World to merchants from five privileged ports: Rouen, La Rochelle, Bordeaux, Saint-Malo, and Nantes. A Nantes slave ship would in these days probably arrive every week in Saint-Domingue.

Beaumarchais was still hopeful of winning this lucrative contract in early 1765. He wrote optimistically to his father: "Everyone is talking of my affair. I am complimented as if it were completed successfully."

Here are some bills which he sent in January to Paris in relation to his scheme:

I pay to M Aralde	5,700,000 reales
I undertake to settle the other debts in relation to the asiento which I make out as	3,000,000 reales
I invest in the provision of grain which I put in the warehouses	6,000,000 reales
I provide the king with a guarantee for the security of the service and I charge myself to pay H.M. what is due for the asiento	6,000,000 reales
Total	20,700,000 reales
Setting up the New Company	20,700,000 reales
My work for the asiento	20,700,000 reales
Further work	27,600,000 reales

From these records it will be seen that Beaumarchais was nearly as skilful with figures as he was with witty sayings.

But in the end, Beaumarchais failed to win this important opportunity. He lost out to Uriarte. The reason was simple: the decisive administrative body, the Council of the Indies, was utterly against handing over this jewel in Spanish commerce to a Frenchman. Conservative-minded members of the council, such as José Pablo de Agüero and Rafael Antúnez y Acevedo, were also hostile to Beaumarchais for personal reasons. They had both served in the Casa de Contratación at Cádiz (the body responsible for trade with the Americas) before they were promoted to the Council of the Indies, and they knew all the merchants of that city. Antúnez's father had also worked in the Casa de Contratación. Another member of the council was José Esteban Abaría, who had been president of the Casa de Contratación and was seen as "an ideal covert agent at court for Cádiz interests." The hostility to France was reflected, too, by the minister for the navy, Julián de Arriaga, who was generally responsible for the colonies, and by his chief civil servant, Pedro de Rada. These officials believed that it was desirable that all trade with the Spanish New World be concentrated in Cádiz rather than in Nantes or Bordeaux.

Miguel de Uriarte was, it is true, obliged to accept certain conditions. Thus he had to undertake to take 1,500 slaves every year to Cartagena de Indias, another 1,500 to Portobelo on the isthmus, and another 1,000 to Havana. Six hundred slaves had also to be carried to Cumaná near Caracas, to Santa Marta on the north coast of South America near Cartagena, to Santo Domingo on Hispaniola, to the island of Trinidad, to Puerto Rico, and to the pearl market in Margarita. A further 400 would have to be taken to both Honduras and Campeche in the Yucatán Peninsula. The disappointed Beaumarchais would not have been comforted by the rumour that Uriarte at this stage, though operating as president of the Cádiz slave company, was really acting on behalf of two English companies.

Beaumarchais was no more successful in pursuing the control of the commerce in Louisiana than he was in respect of the slave trade.

Louisiana had received its name in honour of the Sun King Louis XIV from the explorer and governor La Salle, who sailed down the Mississippi from Illinois in the 1680s. He claimed a territory far larger than the present U.S. state of Louisiana, which perhaps pleased, perhaps astonished, the king. A French colony was founded in 1699, a governor was appointed, and a Louisiana Company established by an adventurous merchant, Antoine Crozat, in 1708. He was granted a monopoly of trade to and from Louisiana. His undertaking was badly managed, but he made enough money to enable his brother Pierre to become the foremost art collector of the age, and his descendant the Duc de Broglie to live as a king. (Broglie would also inherit much of the finance minister Necker's fortune.) Crozat eventually abandoned his interest in Louisiana to the dangerous John Law ("brilliant but fundamentally unsound," as Mr. Tansley in Virginia Woolf's *To the Lighthouse* would have put it), whose Mississippi Company combined with the French East India Company and several other rich trading enterprises to become the Nouvelle Compagnie des Indes, for a time the largest commercial organisation which the world had seen.

Louisiana, meantime, enjoyed a short but delightful era as a new El Dorado, a place where fabulous riches could be obtained. For a time all Frenchmen with ambitions to have money wished to make themselves "Mississippians." The city of New Orleans was founded in 1718, named in honour of Saint-Simon's hero, the then-Regent Orléans. The wealth of the colony survived the fall of John Law, cotton being grown from 1740 and sugar cane from 1751, the clever Jesuits being responsible.

France secretly transferred the colony to Spain in 1762 at the end of the Seven Years' War. The reason for discretion was that Spain thought that the English would seek to penetrate the Spanish empire by trying to expand to Louisiana first, and they believed, probably rightly, that France did not take the defence of the place seriously. The few French colonists hated the change. But an experienced Spanish governor, Antonio de Ulloa, sailed in and the transfer was made public in 1769.

The opportunities of opening trade to the new Spanish colony of Louisiana seemed splendid to Pâris-Duverney, though he was a more cautious financier than Law had been.

The idea of a concession of trade with Louisiana to Beaumarchais and Pâris-Duverney was supported by King Charles III and Grimaldi. They were always partisans of close collaboration with France. But the Council of the Indies was aghast precisely because Beaumarchais's company was French. The same officials in the council (Antúnez, Agüero, Rada) who had opposed the grant of the licence for trading slaves to the French were busy opposing any concession here. After turning down Beaumarchais's request, Grimaldi wrote, "Whatever the proposals which you have made to me for setting up a Louisiana company, they do much honour to your talents and only confirm the good opinion that I had of you. I have, sir, been delighted to have known you and I would like to bear witness to your capacity. If your plans had been compatible with the constitution of Spanish America, I think that their success would have been assured; but we had to give way to insurmountable difficulties opposing them. I would be delighted to be able to render you service on another occasion."

Beaumarchais drew gloomy conclusions from these experiences: he thought that he had been thwarted by the "natural hate that the people of Spain have towards us either because of their inferiority at every level or because of the profound scorn which the French have always shown towards Spanish customs." But he continued to believe that "the love of letters is not incompatible with the spirit of business," as he causes Figaro to insist in *The Barber of Seville* (act I, scene 2).

SEVEN

Madame de Croix

Beaumarchais had thus failed in respect of his attempts at the provisioning of the Spanish army, at financing the proposed colonies in the Sierra Morena, and at securing the right to a monopoly of the slave trade and of commerce in Louisiana. But he had reached what seemed to be a satisfactory resolution of his sister's personal problems. There was one further undertaking to try and settle: Caron, Beaumarchais's father, we recall, was owed money by several people in Madrid.

Most of these were persons of standing in Spain. Thus the Condesa-Duquesa de Benavente, who owed Caron one thousand écus, was María Faustina Girón, daughter of the Duque and Duquesa de Osuna, who had married her elderly husband, Francisco, the fourteenth Conde-Duque de Benavente, when only fourteen in 1738. Her husband's was one of the oldest of Spanish titles: a sixteenth-century ancestor had refused to accept the order of the Golden Fleece from Charles V on the ground that he did not want a foreign honour. Caron's creditor was the mother of the famous aristocrat whom Goya painted with her husband, the Duque de Osuna, and their children in their delightful house outside Madrid, the Alameda de Osuna, now a public park.

The Duquesa de Bournonville, who owed 4,675 livres, was the wife of a nobleman of recent creation. The family, French in origin, had come to Spain with the Bourbons; indeed, King Philip V had granted them their dukedom. The current duke, Francisco Alberto, had been captain of the royal guard, and his chief task had been to attend the king when he went hunting—no sinecure in the reign of Charles III. The Duquesa, like the Condesa-Duquesa de Benavente, was a maid of honour to the queen mother, Elizabeth Farnese. Saint-Simon despised and disliked the first Spanish duke of this name.

Of the Condesa de Uceda, Beaumarchais noted that she was "compliant without my having to demand too much."

The fourth indebted noblewoman was the Condesa de Fuenclara, born María Teresa Patiño, a friend of Caron in her youth, thirty-three years before, in 1731, the year before Beaumarchais had been born. She was now in her sixties, but she had in Madrid a successful salon, a regular tertulia in the French style, in her fine house in the Calle de Hortaleza on the corner of the now disappeared Calle San Miguel and the Calle de la Reina. It was close to the Red de San Luis and so to the home of Beaumarchais's sisters.

Beaumarchais went to see her. Her late husband, Pedro Cebrián y Agustín, fifth Conde de Fuenclara (the title was a creation of the sixteenth century), had been a diplomat in his youth. As ambassador to Dresden and Vienna, he had helped to arrange the ground for the wedding of the present King Charles, then king of Naples, to his late queen, María Amalia of Saxony. From 1742 to 1746 he had been viceroy to Mexico, where he was known for such reforms as the reconstruction of the aqueduct of Chapultepec and the rebuilding of certain streets in the north of the capital, as well as for his difficulties with the English admiral Anson, who spent many months uninvited in Acapulco on his journey round the world. But the countess did not accompany her husband on these distinguished postings.

Another among the debtors was the young Antonio Patiño, third Marqués de Castelar, who was quite ruined. He was a nephew of the Condesa de Fuenclara. His father had been an ambassador and a minister in the 1720s, and he and his brother José had been close advisers of King Philip V. Recently the third marqués's affairs were in such a bad state that he had abandoned Madrid and gone to live in his half-derelict palace in Saragossa.

Another debtor was the Catalan Miguel Ferrer, a banker who had lost everything in recent dealings. His affairs were in chaos, so much so that he apparently could not contemplate anything in the way of payments.

We must assume that all these debts were on account of unpaid bills for watches or clocks made for the persons concerned during visits to Paris at some time in the previous twenty years, although some such timepieces may have been sold by the Caron sisters.

Beaumarchais set about securing the settlement of these debts as if they were an extra challenge to his commercial capacity. The introduction of the Condesa de Fuenclara was a good way to meet the people concerned. But Beaumarchais reported to his father that when she knew of his arrival, the Duquesa de Bournonville took to her bed with smallpox, which "the wits" said derived from his own insistence. The Condesa-Duquesa de Benavente beat about the bush ("tergiverse"), while Señora de Uceda paid up with a bang ("avec une retenue").

The Condesa de Fuenclara invited Beaumarchais to her house several times. Acting as his "good angel," she introduced him to many of her friends. On June 5 two letters reached Beaumarchais from Paris. First, Caron wrote,

> I receive by the same courier two letters from my charming countess, one to me, one to Julie [Beaumarchais's favourite sister]. She writes in such a beautiful and touching way, full of tender expressions for me and honourable ones for you and which you would not have less pleasure than I did when you read them. You have plainly enchanted her. She does not stop saying what a pleasure it is to have met you and to talk of her wish to be useful to you, and how all Spaniards approve your actions in relation to Clavijo. Please, do not neglect her.

The same day Julie wrote: "You are the naughtiest devil that I know, a real monster . . . honour of the family, loved in all the courts. Give me details, we die with impatience. . . . The countess tells us that she loves you madly, she wants me to say whether I would like better something from the Indies or from Spain. I do not know how to choose, I have replied. I want what is most frivolous, or paltry, provided it comes from Her Excellency." In July, Caron wrote again to Beaumarchais telling him again not to neglect the Comtesse de Fuenclara, who had told Caron that she has seen his son only twice.

Among those to whom she introduced Beaumarchais was an admirer of the Marqués de Castelar, her ruined nephew. This was the French Marquesa de Croix, the young wife of a distinguished soldier, Francisco de Croix, Marqués de Croix, now sixty-one, a Fleming in origin. He had been in the Walloon guards, then served in the wars in Italy before becoming governor of Ceuta in North Africa, then governor-general of Andalusia and afterwards of Galicia. A portrait of him a little later shows him as unsmiling and serious, but there is a strong hint of efficacy about his dry lips. He would later have in Mexico a name as an autocrat.

The marquesa for her part was a niece of Monseigneur Louis Sextius Jarente de la Bruyère, bishop of Orléans, who had earlier enjoyed the see of Digne. (From a reference to her in the Marqués's will, her first name seems to have been Fernanda or Fernande.) The bishop's *maitresse-en-titre* at that time was Madame de Croix's elder sister, his niece. The bishop was a good-looking man, amiable and jovial, of a witty and naïve gaiety, sweet in character but with an easy manner. He was also a friend and follower of Choiseul, who liked wits.

Baron Gleichen, the Danish minister in Madrid, seems to be the only person to have written of Madame de Croix in a memoir. He wrote without restraint that "she has what one calls a Roman beauty but so perfect that one really has never seen her equal. She has a figure full of grace and character. Her eyes are piercing and her nose aquiline, her head high and proud, a superb carriage; in a word she is the ideal of a good empress." A Roman empress, one supposes.

Her uncle, Monseigneur de Jarente, had sent letters of recommendation for Madame de Croix to ministers Grimaldi and Squillace, as to the French ambassador, the Marquis de Ossun, when she came to Spain. Why did she need them when she was, after all, married to the governor-general of Galicia? Perhaps, as Maurice Lever has speculated, she was a secret agent of the king of France, who had other such ladies in his service. French diplomacy in the eighteenth century abounded with such people. Lever calls her "an adventuress." Yet the Jarentes were an old family in Provence.

When Croix left for Galicia as governor-general, he left his beautiful wife, for no reason that anyone could understand, in her hometown, Avignon. She responded by managing her family's property, Sénas, having, as the baron Gleichen rather tartly put the matter, nothing better to do. She was also taken up by the papal vice legate to Avignon, Monseigneur Pascuale Acquaviva, from the

Abruzzi, who fell in love with her. Acquaviva, whose surname is a very well-known one in ecclesiastical history, was, recalled Baron Gleichen, "candid but very fat." Cervantes had worked for a time with a Cardinal Acquaviva in 1569.

Madame de Croix seems also to have been adored by the Marqués de Castelar, and perhaps indeed it was in her cause that he ruined himself.

The Marqués de Croix did not seem to be affected by these friendships of his wife. After all, the custom of fashionable women having *cortejos*—gallants attached to them—was by then well established in Spain. A character in a *sainete* declared that to look for conjugal fidelity at that time was to look for a cat with three legs. A later French ambassador, Bourgoing, asserted at the end of the eighteenth century that there were no people in Europe among whom fewer jealous husbands were to be found than in Spain. Jealousy, he thought, was a fable "withdrawn from circulation [in Spain] at the beginning of the century." The English traveller the Reverend Joseph Townsend wrote that a husband would often not be invited to his wife's tertulias in Madrid in those days. What kind of conversation the marqués ever had with his wife is a mystery. He was a hard, determined autocrat, as his administration in Mexico showed. She was light-hearted, charming, decorative, with mysterious depths. Perhaps they were well matched.

Madame de Croix probably met Beaumarchais in July 1764. They had evidently become very friendly by August. Beaumarchais wrote to his father from La Granja—on the twelfth of that month:

There is here in the room where I am writing a tall and beautiful woman who is a great friend of your dear countess [de Fuenclara] who makes fun of both you and me daily. She [La Fuenclara] says to me, for example, that she thanks you for the kindness that you showed her thirty-three years ago, when you laid the foundation of the friendly relations which I have had for two months with her. I have assured her that I shall not fail to write to you and, on this instant, I shall do it, because this is only a joke on her part in order to give me pleasure by saying everything that she really thinks.

Here the Marquesa de Croix added, in her own hand, "I think it, I feel it, I sense it, and I swear it, Monsieur." Presumably, that meant that she agreed with what Beaumarchais had said.

Beaumarchais concluded, "Do not fail, through any sense of seemliness, in your next letter, to thank Her Excellency [La Fuenclara] for *her* thanks and still more for the courtesies with which she covers me. I swear to you that, without the charm of such attractive society, my Spanish life would be full of bitterness."

There were several other references to the Marquesa de Croix in the letters of Beaumarchais that summer: for example, on August 19, 1764, from the royal palace at La Granja he wrote:

On my return to Madrid, I shall see your dear countess since she is very angry with me [for not having been to see her recently]. I have talked of it to Madame de Croix, who is her great friend and whose society dissipates all dust, inaction, boredom, impatience but which I do not feel when writing to you because she is just outside. My favourite maxim is that one should not sacrifice the future to the present nor the present to the future, I swear to you that I would be dead in this *real,* this dull *sitio* [a *sitio real* in Spanish is a royal possession], without the delicious company that my angel [La Fuenclara] has procured for me, since it has connected me with the most beautiful and witty of French women who surpasses all possible Spaniards.

The court, having been at Aranjuez from Easter till the end of July, would normally go in those days for the rest of the summer to La Granja. That had once been a farm belonging to the Jeronymite monks and had been transformed by Charles III's French father, King Philip V, into a grand chateau in the style of Versailles. "They have cost me three millions and amused me three minutes," King Philip is supposed to have remarked about the fountains. But those fountains were actually superior to those of Versailles, and the sight of the gardens was held by a much later French ambassador to be a reason alone for going to Spain. Deer wandered in the park and were safe except for the one day in October when the king organised a shoot. Beaumarchais reached there in early August 1764 and was still there, as was the court, at the end of September.

For much of this time he was accompanied by the Marquesa de Croix. His relation to her is not quite clear. It is obvious that he loved her company. But was she his mistress? All Beaumarchais's biographers have assumed so. Nothing proves it absolutely, and, as will be seen, his conduct towards her was not always that of a lover.

All the same, a year later, Beaumarchais, back in Paris, wrote to the banker Durand in Madrid asking him to go and see the marquesa: "Ensure on my behalf not to neglect to tell me anything agreeable which occurs to her. My knowledge of and affection for her are the two columns of my existence about which I shall write nothing further." That sounds as if the relation was one of love. To the same banker Beaumarchais wrote a little later, "I beg you to assure Madame la Marquesa de Croix of my most tender and respectful attachment."

One other piece of evidence should be considered: the outstanding biographer of Beaumarchais in the nineteenth century was Louis de Loménie. In the introduction to volume one of his two-volume biography published in 1856, he says that he had found, in a box of papers and family objects, devoted to Beaumarchais's life, some portraits of women. One of them was a miniature representing a beautiful woman of twenty or twenty-five years of age, wrapped in a paper carrying the words, in a fine but rather scrawled handwriting, "I give you back my portrait." Loménie wrote that he recognised the handwriting as being of 1764 and then he quoted the famous, haunting words of the poet Jacques Villon, "Où sont les neiges d'antan?"—Where are the snows of yesteryear?

On the other hand, Beaumarchais then did something which seems, at least to us of the twenty-first century, to be the action of an ambitious cynic, rather than of a lover. He had cultivated the friendship of the king's valet, Amerigo Pini. Pini was, as we have learned, the chief confidant of Charles III. Pini, "crafty and Italian," as Beaumarchais put it, had thought that he would try and find the king a mistress. That surely would secure for him the king's gratitude. Perhaps the king would give him an island, as Don Quixote was always promising Sancho Panza would happen at the end of their adventures. Casanova might say, "Evil be to him who suggests to him—the king—a mistress." But the Italian Pini thought that a lady would humanise his master.

Beaumarchais had a better idea. He wanted to arrange that this mistress would be not only a clever woman but one who would work secretly for France and thereby be "an underpinning of the Pacte de Famille." Madame de Croix was Beaumarchais's choice. He arranged to show her off to Pini, pretending to seek alternatives and then to light on her by chance. He told Pini that, after careful reflection, he found her to satisfy all the conditions, and said that he would take it on himself to persuade her to go ahead with the dangerous if fascinating scheme. Pini agreed and went through with the king the same procedure that he, Beaumarchais, had undertaken with Pini, seeming to suggest others and then to light on the beautiful French girl as if by chance.

Beaumarchais talked to Madame de Croix. He worked seriously to try and make the idea seem attractive to a woman of wit who was also, he pointed out in a subsequent note to Choiseul, ambitious, and who wanted to improve the finances of her debt-ridden husband, the marqués. Beaumarchais argued that her presence would assist the so-much-to-be-desired enlightened reforms in Spain. He insisted that she would at the same time be serving France. He flattered her *amour-propre* and cultivated the romance in her head in pointing out the glorious consequences which could follow a liaison with the benign king. When she trembled at the thought of being all alone in this endeavour, Beaumarchais insisted that she could comfort herself by beginning a secret correspondence with Choiseul, still the first minister in France, so maintaining the close friendship of the two countries and helping to conserve their allegiance against the English for whom she had "the most cordial hatred."

The marquesa at first objected that to embark on a scandalous life with the king clashed with both her principles and her tastes. The king, after all, was unattractive. Had not his first cousin once removed, Madame Adélaïde, the daughter of King Louis XV and one of Beaumarchais's patronesses, refused to think of marrying him when she saw his portrait? He might not be as unappealing as his brother the licentious Infante Luis, but that was not saying much.

Perhaps the beautiful marquesa was a French agent. Perhaps that was her raison d'être. Beaumarchais later gave his minister, the engaging Choiseul, a complicated explanation in his *Mémoire d'Espagne:*

> I persuaded her entirely by assuring her that, far from making her enter upon any forgetfulness of duties in relation to

myself [that is, to continue being Beaumarchais's mistress, we assume], I had only set eyes upon her to be certain that such a thing would never happen. I proved to her that the king, feeble and pious, could at any moment be dragged away from pleasure by remorse, for any edifice founded on "a vicious liaison" might fall apart at the first dispute with the confessor. Instead of a severity sweetened by the charms of an agreeable society, and a union founded on mutual esteem and sustained by the respect she would inspire in the king, it would lead to a more sure way of governing him, more than a weakness which would put him always at war with his conscience.

Beaumarchais thus saw himself as governing Spain in the interests of France through the agency of his own friend, whom he would share with the king. No doubt we should remember that at that time, in the words of Theodore Besterman, the biographer of Voltaire, "rare were the women of . . . rank who were content with one lover at a time." Perhaps Beaumarchais was again influenced in his conduct by the example of Pâris-Duverney, who had helped to secure the place in the French court of Madame de Pompadour, who, according to Casanova, may have been his niece. The historian Albert Sorel thought that "to provide a mistress for a King was one of the main devices of diplomacy in the eighteenth century."

The valet Pini told Beaumarchais that the king soon noticed the marquesa in the crowd at court. Once the king had taken in her beauty, he and Pini began to spend every evening talking about her and speculating of what might come to pass. At last, apparently conquered by desire and wanting Pini to embark on a negotiation with Madame de Croix, the king asked the valet to write to her and ask her to come and see him at La Granja, where the court still was. The excuse for the meeting was that Madame de Croix could then herself put to the king a request for justice in relation to some debts of her husband, at that time still serving in Galicia. Beaumarchais, being with the marquesa in Madrid, persuaded her to leave "sur-le champ."

But as soon as the king had the marquesa at his side, unease began to torment him. He gave her a rendezvous to see him in private, but then cancelled the assignation. This happened about ten times. Beaumarchais commented: "Like children to whom a sudden terror prevents from abandoning themselves to what they have most wanted, the king, when a natural opportunity appeared of seeing the lady whom he loved, found more and more reasons to avoid reaching the moment that he had taken such care to inspire; he seemed unable to break out of a kind of suffocation without experiencing a profound sadness."

All these symptoms of a grand passion, Beaumarchais wrote, judged as such by Pini as well as by himself, "determined us to seize on the first order which he gave, to bring her immediately to the king without giving him time to change his mind again; but then I told the lady to refuse absolutely the king's approaches in order that he would become more occupied by our (her) refusals than by his own irresolution, so that his passion would increase because of the difficulty of satisfying it."

This complicated manoeuvre seemed to work. The king first asked the marquesa to try and arrange for herself to be recommended directly to him by the king of France, his first cousin. She had already been recommended, as we have seen, by Choiseul and others in Paris. Then King Charles did something which astonished the court and the ministers: he recommended that the Marqués de Croix should immediately receive the order of Santiago, while he presented the marquesa with a pension, as well as a cross of magnificent diamonds which had been given to him by his brother, the voluptuary Don Luis. She would, too, be named a lady of honour to the future new princess of Asturias, the future Queen María Luisa (a granddaughter of Louis XV), who would marry the Infante Carlos the following year.

On October 28, 1764, Beaumarchais wrote to his father saying that he and his two sisters had been present at the presentation by the king to the Marqués de Croix of the order of Santiago. That was already an honorary order but it was none the less much coveted. For Croix it was a recognition of the favour of the king, even if it was a more conventional prize than what Beaumarchais had conceived for his wife. For though as a maid of honour the marquesa could and would henceforth be seen regularly by the king, nothing further transpired. Thus Beaumarchais's dazzling scheme did not lead him, after all, to becoming indirectly, through the embraces of the marquesa, the master of Spain.

It would seem likely that, whatever had happened before, Madame de Croix became the mistress of Beaumarchais after the failure of his attempt to bring the king into his plot. Beaumarchais probably did not meet the marquesa till July. We know that the drama with the king occurred at La Granja. The Court was there as a rule between June and October. Beaumarchais's "attachment," as he put it, to the marquesa probably began at latest in October after the king had made his decision to remain celibate.

EIGHT

Life in Madrid

The Spanish court customarily went to the Escorial at the beginning of October and stayed there until about December 10. This move was to the great Jeronymite monastery, about four hours from Madrid. It was the site from which King Philip II had ruled Spain and his great empire. (It later became a home for the Augustinians, who established a famous school there.)

When the court arrived at El Escorial, the monastery would be transformed; the two hundred monks would all move to the south and west wings, leaving their cells to the king and the nobility. The rest of the court, the civil servants and the maids, would cram themselves into lodgings or inns in the nearby village. The playlet (*sainete*) of Ramón de la Cruz called "La Fonda del Escorial" gave a vivid picture of the uncomfortable life there.

There was a great library in the monastery which Beaumarchais visited, and where he looked at a large and ancient Petrarch. He told the Duc de la Vallière all about it, because of his interest in books. The visit filled him with anxiety: "One of the things which struck me most in this magnificent monastery is the condemnation of the books of almost all our modern philosophers which is pasted up in the monks' choir. The banned books are named by author and title, and in particular there are condemned not only all the books of your friend Voltaire but anything which he writes in future."

Back in Madrid, Beaumarchais now sought a full life. Pâris-Duverney's money made it possible: sixty thousand livres was a handsome sum. He started giving "charming supper parties." When he was not "at home" himself, he might ride in the Prado with Lord Rochford, the British ambassador, in his fine coach. That uneven path was much less of a grand avenue than it became a few years later as the Salon del Prado, when the architect Ventura Rodríguez laid out the place as a park and put beautiful fountains there, but already people went there to show themselves off in their coaches. The Prado had been renowned in Spanish comedy and romance as a place for intrigue, and robbery. A stream ran down the centre of it and orange sellers, lime sellers, and hazelnut women plied their trades—sometimes, it would seem, secretly carrying messages from lovers in one coach to those in another. There were many beggars. In Beaumarchais's *The Barber of Seville,* the Count of Almaviva is caused to meet his future countess, Rosine, here: "Please be aware," Almaviva says to Figaro, "that chance caused me to meet in the

Prado six months ago a young person of a beauty you cannot imagine. . . . You are going to see her" (act I, scene 4). It was here too—if at the northern end near where there would soon be the admirable fountain accompanying the statue of Cibeles, goddess of fertility—that some fifteen years before the Italian painter Antonio Jolli had depicted the great Calle Alcalá with marvellous warmth.

Beaumarchais went to tertulias in private houses and also attended some private concerts, such as those given by his new friend the British ambassador, Lord Rochford, who was a Dutchman in origin, being descended from an illegitimate son of one of the Stadtholders. This nobleman was extravagant—so much so that, when he left Madrid, he had to pawn his silver. One of his follies had been to order a superb dinner service with his coat of arms in the centre. His motto was "Spes durat avorum" (The hope of my forebears endures) but the painter had mistakenly written "Spes durat amorum" (The hope of love lasts) which was more in keeping with his wild private life. (Rochford was later ambassador in Paris and later still joined the unsuccessful cabinet of the Duke of Grafton as secretary of state for the northern department.) Horace Walpole and Choiseul thought him foolish, but Beaumarchais considered him astute.

In these months, Beaumarchais was often, or so he assured his sister Julie, the life and soul of the party. It being winter, there would probably have been dancing at the gatherings to which he went: directed by a *bastonero*, a master of ceremonies, chosen at random from among the guests, who had to be well informed to cope with the desires and prejudices of his fellow dancers. The music might be provided by a band of blind performers playing guitars, violins, flutes, or oboes, and even horns and bass viols. Such dances in those days were usually begun and brought to an end by minuets (often danced with hats on), and there would also be such old favourites as *contradanzas*, as well as dances which had a strong element of play. There was, for example, a dance called the *meona* in which the dancers, in a ring, having previously taken a mouthful of water, would spit into the middle of the circle. The "Chinese march" obliged the dancers to go on all fours. Beaumarchais was very good at all these, at least according to his own account, and there is no reason to doubt his word.

He also went to public dances which were more scandalous, in so-called "*bailes de candil*," lit only by rough lamps. These were really early nightclubs. The door was open to anyone who wanted to enter, especially *majos* and *majas*, a most curious social phenomenon. These were working-class fops who dressed themselves up to the nines and affected a most elaborate courtesy. Some of these when dancing would perform wild gestures which shocked even Beaumarchais. The most alarming dance, he thought, was the *fandango*, danced by two people who never touch one another but expressed all the gestures involved in lovemaking.

He wrote to the Duc de la Vallière:

Normal dancing is absolutely unknown here, by which I mean the figured dance, because I don't give this name to the grotesque and often indecent movements of the dances from Granada, or Moorish dances, which delight these people. The most popular here is something called the fandango, whose music has an extreme vivacity and whose entire amusement consists in making lascivious paces or movements. . . . Even I, who am not the most modest of men, could not help blushing.

A young Spanish girl without lifting her eyes and with a modest figure gets up in order to place herself before a worldly man-about-town. She begins by extending her arms to snap her fingers: which she continues to do throughout the fandango to mark the time; then the man turns, he seems to distance himself, he returns with several violent movements to which she replies with similar gestures, although a little more sweet and always with those snapping fingers which seem to be saying: "I am laughing at you, go where you like, it will not be I who tires first." There are duchesses and other very distinguished ladies whose enthusiasm is limitless for the fandango.

The taste for this obscene dance, which we might perhaps compare with the "*calenda*" [as described vividly by Father Jean-Baptiste Labal] of our Negroes in America, is very well established in these people.

Even Casanova was surprised, if more pleased than was Beaumarchais, by this exhibition when he reached Madrid a few years later:

"What I liked best about the spectacle," he wrote of a masked ball, "was a wonderful and fantastic dance which struck up at midnight ... the famous fandango. .... Each couple dances only three steps, but the gestures and the attitudes are the most lascivious imaginable. Everything is represented, from the first expression of desire to the final ecstasy. It is a true history of love. I could not conceive a woman refusing her partner anything after this dance, for it seems to stir the senses. I was so excited at the bacchanalian spectacle that I burst into cries of delight."

The fandango had a part in polite society. Thus in the contemporary playlet "Las Resultas de los Saraos," which might be translated "The hangover," a lady named Guerrera is made to ask, "Will there be also a fandango tonight?" Granadina answers, "Certainly. I hope it will go on till morning." A little later Granadina asks the Gallego water carrier, "And to-day, what will you be eating?" "Fandangu," was the Gallego's answer.

Another dance was the *seguidilla,* usually performed by four couples to the music of a guitar and castanets. This dance was accompanied by a singer who often sang strophes of four verses, with a refrain. There were many kinds of seguidillas, such as *manchegas, andaluzas, seguidillas gitanas,* and *seguidillas boleras.* The last named eventually became the bolero, which continues to have its passionate devotees. All these dances had distinct movements quite different from each other, which were carefully learned by nobility and populace alike.

Beaumarchais wrote the words to a seguidilla and accompanied them on a guitar: "Even though I laugh," he wrote to his sister in Paris,

> I could send you verses written for your *serviteur* for these Spanish seguidillas, which are very pretty vaudevilles but with words which are usually worthless. One says here, as in Italy, the words are nothing, the music is everything. ... But one moment, gentlemen, don't let the gaiety of the night spoil the work of the morning. So I continue as always, I write and I think of business matters all day and, in the evening, I give myself up to the pleasures of a society as enlightened as it is well chosen.

> Receive the last seguidilla which comes from my quiver. It is one which has been most successful here. It is in the hands of everyone here who speaks French. I have written the words as if for a shepherdess who reaches her rendezvous first and complains at the man who is making her wait. The words are:

> *The vows of lovers*
> *Are light as wind, their sweetness*
> *Are deceiving traps*
> *Hidden beneath flowers.*
> *Yesterday, Lindor, in a charming rapture*
> *Swore to me again*
> *that his sighs*
> *his desires are awoken by the expectation of pleasure . . .*

"My dear Boisgarnier," he added, using one of the nicknames which the Caron family enjoyed, "I am going to drink some syrup of maidenhair because, for three days, I have had a frightful cold in the head, but I envelop myself in my Spanish cloak with a good highwayman's hat on my head; it's what one calls here 'capa y sombrero,' and, when a man throws his cloak on his shoulder, he can hide a portion of his face so he is called '*embossado*,' disguised."

"Lindor," here supposed by Beaumarchais to be the shepherdess's friend, was the name which was an alias for the Count of Almaviva in act I, scene 2, of *The Barber of Seville*, and it often turns up in pastoral plays or tales of the time: for example, in the story of Marmontel, *Le Scrupule*, written in 1761. Sir Walter Scott once demanded: "For heaven's sake, do not bring down Corydon and Lindor on us." Beaumarchais had a Lindor in his unfinished playlet "The Sacristan," written when he returned to Paris after 1765.

As to other visits in Madrid, Beaumarchais would surely have gone to the headquarters of the Royal Academy of Fine Arts, at that time on the second floor of the long building known as the Panadería in the Plaza Mayor. That seventeenth-century square, comparable to the Place du Marais, was occasionally used for executions. Its windows were closed during executions. If there were an execution by garrote, the scaffold would be near the Portal de Paños; if by hanging or beheading it would be at the Carnicería, the meat market.

The Plaza Mayor was also used as a market, where—especially, as today, at Christmas time—there were many types of pious illustrations, including many cribs, as well as loud-shouting turkey sellers, knife grinders from Galicia or France, oil sellers (calling "Oil, oil!"), and good-looking women selling chestnuts.

Beaumarchais does not seem to have gone to any tavern, inn, or wine shop (except for the dark rooms where he saw the fandangos), nor to the bullring beyond the Puerta de Alcalá, which had been built ten years before by the late King Ferdinand VI. King Charles III, like his father King Philip V, disliked bullfights. If Beaumarchais had gone to a corrida, he, coming from a country which loves dogs, might have found the then-frequent use of dogs in the ring most disturbing.

Beaumarchais was still in Madrid at Christmas 1764. He wrote to the Duc de la Vallière on Christmas Eve that it seemed "the most complete Roman saturnalia. The uncontrollable licence reigning in the churches in the name of joy is incredible. There is a church where even the monks dance in the choir with castanets. The people perform *paroli* (a complicated musical game) with cauldrons, whistles, balloons, tapdancing (*claquettes*), and drums. Then there are the cries, the songs, the dangerous jumps, everything in the style of a fair, the bacchanale filling the streets all night: for eight days there was a sung Mass accompanied by the infernal faburden [choral harmonisation] in a church just next to me, and all in honour of the birth of Christ, who was the most tranquil and wise of men."

On the last day of 1764, the king moved his principal Madrid residence from the old Palacio del Retiro east of the city to the new palace built in the west by the Italian architect Sabatini. This was on the ruins of the old Alcázar, which had been accidentally burned down in 1734. It was very grand and lasted as the home of the kings till the temporary overthrow of the Spanish monarchy in 1931. Napoleon, walking there with his brother Joseph, whom he had established on the Spanish throne in 1808, remarked to him, "You will be much better lodged than I in France."

NINE

At the Tables and to the Theatre

Reading between the lines of Beaumarchais's letters in these months, it would seem that Madame de Croix was usually with him at that time as his companion. She was certainly with Beaumarchais when he won a fortune at brelan against the ambassador of Russia, Peter, Count of Buturlin.

Brelan was an old simple game in which each player is dealt three cards, on which he bets. Three aces, the best hand, was known as a brelan.

In the past, gambling in Spain had been condemned, and playing for money considered heresy. But many Neapolitans came to Spain with King Charles III determined to gamble, and though the law still included such punishments for gambling as banishment to the country for five years, a fine of two hundred ducats, even a hundred strokes with the whip, secret gambling prevailed. Smart tertulias were especially arranged for the hostess to profit by gambling, pocketing her gains, for example, and avoiding paying if she lost. There was thus apparently gambling every night at the house of the Condesa-Duquesa de Benavente, one of Caron's debtors, where a secretary of the Inquisition and a ruined merchant were that winter the most frequent players.

Buturlin had been in his youth a soldier, like so many diplomats at that time. His father had reached the summit of the Russian political ladder as a field marshal, as governor of the Ukraine, and then as a count. His second wife, the ambassador's mother, was a Princess Kuratin, from one of the main political dynasties of old Russia. The younger Buturlin had a pretty wife, María Romanovna, Countess Vorontsova, a sister of Princess Catherine Dashkova, the best friend of the Empress Catherine and, at least according to her own exciting account, the motor of Catherine's dramatic coup d'état in 1762 against her husband Tsar Peter III. (The empress and the twenty-year-old Princess Dashkova, dressed as guards officers and riding astride their horses, rallied the guard against Peter with astonishing panache.) Another sister, Elizabeth Vorontsova, afterwards Madame Paliansky, had been Tsar Peter's ugly mistress. Princess Dashkova would later write a famous memoir.

Russians give a touch of class to any gambling table, and there was nothing to prevent a diplomat gambling all night if he so wished. The ambassador's wife, María, had, according to her sister's memoir, been "very early distinguished by the favour of the em-

press [Elizabeth] and even when still a child had been appointed
a maid of honour." This was the age when for the first time Russia
was beginning to count as a major European power: "sprung from
those Huns and Gepides who destroyed the empire of the East,"
Frederick the Great would in 1769 write to his brother Henry, "they
could well break into the empire of the West before long." One had
to take Russian diplomats seriously.

Early in February 1765, Beaumarchais played against the Buturlins jointly and won two thousand livres from them. They did
not pay. Probably that was because they believed that it was not
necessary to settle debts incurred in one's own house. Similar games
continued over several weeks. Then Buturlin won one hundred louis,
but he still did not pay anything back nor indeed did he speak of
doing so. Beaumarchais said: "If the count lends me some money,
I shall embark on a folly and take the bank." He did take the bank
and lost money to Lord Rochford, the British ambassador, to the
Duque de San Blas—and to Buturlin. To the latter, Beaumarchais
said, "Ah, my dear count, we are quits." The count said that what he
owed could not be balanced against what the bank should pay him.
"That," he said, "does not really cost you anything." "That's what
you could say to me," returned Beaumarchais, "if I had been a bad
debtor." At that, Madame de Croix got up and told Beaumarchais
to give her his arm. They left.

The next stages in the dispute were somewhat disagreeable.
Beaumarchais and Madame de Croix went back to the Russian
embassy, as was normal for them, in order to avoid giving the

impression that they were angry. Beaumarchais lost every night about 10 or 12 louis, against a bank of 200, but before he left he developed the custom of putting all he gained on two cards, which always won. He broke the bank when it was in the hands of the Marqués de Carassola. The Chevalier de Guzmán put 500 louis on the table and said, "Gentlemen, don't go, I wish to bet that Monsieur de Beaumarchais will break the new bank." Beaumarchais felt obliged to accept the bet, having already made 200 louis. Everyone watched, because no one else played for such high stakes as he did. He put ten louis on each of his three cards. He was dealt three aces, a brelan, so he doubled his winnings. He continued to win and, in two hours, he broke the bank again. He went to bed having made 500 louis, of which next day he lost 150. Thinking then that he had played enough, he was about to go home when Buturlin came up and said to him, "Is it possible that you are not going to play against me?" "I have lost a great deal this evening," said Beaumarchais. "But yesterday you won more," said the diplomat. In the end they played, and Beaumarchais won another 200 louis. He again sought to leave. Again the Russian insisted that the game continue, though it was four in the morning. Beaumarchais insisted on giving up, and the Countess Buturlin, angry at the losses of her husband, said to him, "You are more fortunate than polite, monsieur." "Madame," he said, "you forget that eight days ago, when dining with Lord Rochford, you said quite the contrary." For at the British embassy, the Countess Buturlin had begged him to lend her 30 louis to pay what she owed at one of the tables.

For several days, Beaumarchais and Madame de Croix kept their distance from the Buturlins. They were missed. The Russian residence lost all its charm in Beaumarchais's absence. Beautiful Madrileñas, Beaumarchais wrote home to Paris, tried to persuade him to go back. The count then sent him, care of Madame de Croix, the money that he owed without a word of apology for the delay. The Countess Buturlin in the end sent her doctor to Beaumarchais and begged him to return. He did not respond. Finally Buturlin sent a persuasive Russian friend, Prince Mezersky, to invite Beaumarchais: there would also be a concert, then a supper. Beaumarchais yielded. He arrived late, finding the countess at the harpsichord. When she saw Beaumarchais coming in, she stopped playing; there was total silence. She then said, "Monsieur, friends such as you and Monsieur de Buturlin should never quarrel because of vulgar misunderstandings. We both hope that you will do us the honour to remain." The countess added, "Monsieur de Beaumarchais, I have a plan to play Annette in the play of Marmontel, *Annette et Lubin.* I hope that you will agree to play the part of Lubin, and the Swedish minister will play the lord. Prince Mezersky will be the magistrate. We are already in rehearsal." Beaumarchais accepted. The play was performed, the actors reading their parts. Afterwards there was music and a sumptuous supper. Buturlin and Beaumarchais each undertook that they would never again talk of brelan, much less play it, nor of faro nor any other such game. At dessert, the countess Buturlin read aloud some lines which she had composed that day in honour of her French guest:

O you to whom nature has arranged to share
The talent of charming as well as a wisdom rare,
If, like Orpheus, you tell a flattering story
Pluto would certainly bring you glory.

"Good God!" concluded Beaumarchais to himself, "These are no ordinary honours. . . . My friendship is closer than ever. The dinner, the concert, more gambling, and I leave with 14,500 livres."

He was later accused anonymously and falsely of having tricked Buturlin out of 100,000 livres.

When in Madrid, Beaumarchais often went to the theatre. He particularly liked the burlesque, racy, impressions of life in Spain to be found in so-called *sainetes*. Indeed, when he returned to Paris, his first writing seems to have been a sainete of his own, "The Sacristan"—whose main character is a seducer, not a clergyman. In a long letter of Christmas 1764 to the Duc de la Vallière, Beaumarchais wrote that music in Spain, unlike the theatre, "could be ranked immediately after Italian music and before ours—the warmth and the gaiety of the interludes, all in music, separating the boring acts of their insipid dramas, and very often making up for those: they are called *tonadillas* and *sainetes*."

A tonadilla was a satirical song usually sung by the actresses of the main play. Sometimes the songs were merely amusing. But they might have a simple plot, such as the love of a gypsy girl for an innkeeper. Later still, they had known composers, and the names of Blas de Laserna and Esteve were famous in this respect in the latter half of the century. Well-known singers would perform, such as Teresa Garrido, the first actress to accompany herself alone on her guitar.

A sainete, on the other hand, was a one-act play with a comic element dominating. The word apparently comes from the expression for the marrow of the bone, or the brains, of a bird killed by a falcon and afterwards given to the raptor as a "titbit." The word at first meant any short play, but by 1760 it signified a playlet, usually in verse, performed in the interval of other plays. The characters were often of the working class and reflected the reality of Spanish society in a witty way.

In those days there were two theatres in Madrid: first, the Coliseo de la Cruz, a stone's throw from the Puerta del Sol, where plays were performed in an open court (*corral*). This had been re-built some twenty years before under the direction of the architect Pedro de Ribera, a disciple of the much more famous but long dead Churriguera. The second theatre, the Corral del Príncipe, not far away, was on the east side of what is today the Plaza de Santa Ana but stood then in front of the Convento de Santa Ana, which housed barefoot Carmelites.

Entry into the Príncipe could be disagreeable: the first disap-pointment was the entrance. One had to pass through a narrow, funnel-like passage which, though only three yards long, had two successive gates where two distinct fees were paid (there were no tickets). The great waves of people, the intense heat, the foul odour that emanated from contiguous lavatories and at times from the crowd itself, the water seller who frequently appeared with his jars forcing his way through the multitude, molesting hundreds of people, stifled and sickened one.

When he went to one of these two theatres, Beaumarchais would have sat in a box, not with the rowdy *mosqueteros* (standing spectators), in the pit, nor yet in the stalls or in the seats raised around the stage in a half-circle. If he went to the Coliseo de la Cruz, Beaumarchais would also have had to endure the sharp tongue of the haughty chief attendant, Francisca Gallego. Many were reluctant to go to that theatre merely because they did not wish to expose themselves to the violent commentary of that lady on their clothes, their face, or their demeanour.

A performance at a theatre would last about three hours, usually starting at 4 P.M. The first act of the main play would be followed by an interval in which a tonadilla would be sung and a sainete might be performed also. There would follow the second act of the play and then another tonadilla or another sainete before the third act.

In the 1760s the outstanding writer of these sainetes was Ramón de la Cruz, a man of Beaumarchais's age who seems to have been a dependent of the Duque de Alba. He was immensely productive, and during the months that Beaumarchais was in Madrid ten new plays of his were presented. Thus there was "El Sarao" (The party), about a picnic in the outskirts of the capital; "Las Resultas de los Saraos" (The hangover), in which the picnickers recover from excessive indulgence; and "La Bella Madre" (The beautiful mother), in which a society lady is brought to accept that she cannot be allowed to commit murder, justifiable though it sometimes seems. "El Caballero de Medina" (The gentleman from Medina) is about a girl whose marriage cannot go ahead. "La Devoción Engañosa" (Deceitful devotion) concerns a lay sister who likes singing tonadillas, while "Las Frioleras" (The baubles) shows a lord of the manor disconcerted by numerous accidents in his town, which he has been showing to a friend as an example of tranquillity. In most of these plays there appear petimetres, majos and majas, clowns, carpenters, apprentices, hairdressers, mayors, and notaries, and also doctors, chemists, councillors, and priests. Which of these plays was seen by Beaumarchais we do not know. But he seems certainly to have been present at a production of "El Celoso Decepcionado" (The deceived jealous husband), by a later famous administrator, Pablo Olavide; and he surely also saw Ramón de la Cruz's "El Barbero" (The barber), which María Ladvenant put on in the summer of 1764.

The outstanding actress at the time was this golden-haired María Ladvenant, "la divina." That star would give her supporters—the *chorizos*—golden silk ribbons. Ladvenant was still only in her middle twenties. She had begun to appear on the stage in Madrid in 1759, and she performed in every kind of play. She was looked on as scandalous; she had narrowly escaped prison, married, and then quickly and sensationally separated from her husband.

"El Barbero" begins with a barber sitting in his shop singing an "air of *fólia*," a song of the Canary Islands, to a guitar. This runs:

How many in their frenzy
Who weep to get a "yes" that they will adore
Know that there are others
Who weep for having said "yes"?
Ay, Love, do not boast of your arrows
Which the bow never snubs
When successful hits are so few
And so certain the many ravages caused.

The song goes on to remind the playgoers that the world is like a wheel, which carries some up and others down. Fortune rules human destiny. There is no lawsuit which a rich man loses which does not make someone else rich. What a contrasting pair of heads they are, the world and fortune! The barber says, "I spend my life crying four times and singing once, thus passing my life avoiding the sticky simplicity of love." His lady is Manuela, and he sighs

¡Ay, imposible Manuela!
¡Ay Manuela! . . .

That was an anticipation of a song still popular in Spain.

Then six gallants appear, one after another, each of whom needs treatment, including bleeding, because of some mistake in love. Next a father comes in. He is trying to disinherit his six daughters because his wife has died and he has married again. The second wife insists that she can do what she likes with the house in which they all live, and also that she will not have anyone playing a guitar there. The house, she declares, belongs to her and her family, and her husband must put up with it, arranging his needs as best he can. The six stepdaughters make a sad entrance, dressed rather dowdily. But they cheer up when their father says that the arrival of a troop of soldiers in the town will bring them husbands. They prepare to welcome the soldiers with a seguidilla. The words are direct:

> *You are very welcome,*
> *Very welcome you are,*
> *To capture souls,*
> *Whom you liberate.*
> *You are very welcome*
> *Very welcome you are.*

These "husbands," however, turn out to be the very gallants whom the barber has been treating for the infirmities of love. He can now provide them with brides, who argue that the dowry of their dead mother must remain with them. This conclusion is managed by the omnicompetent barber, who anticipates the equally efficient creation of Beaumarchais, the barber Figaro, who was to be both more and less than a normal barber.

The tone of Ramón de la Cruz's sainetes was exactly what Beaumarchais later adopted in his own plays.

TEN

Leaving Madrid

On March 22, 1765, Beaumarchais at last left Madrid for Paris. He travelled in a cabriolet driven by a hard-drinking coachman called Vidal, who had been a cook to his sisters. Otherwise he was alone. The first day out, he covered about sixty miles. He met in the Sierra de Guadarrama "the devil's own cold in these frightful mountains, where we have met all kinds of dangers from robbers, ghosts, infuriated wolves."

The second day, they travelled only a very short distance. But on the third day, they covered what Beaumarchais termed "eighty terrible miles," travelling from 5 A.M. till nightfall. Then at a pueblo called Audícana (or Audikana in Basque) some ten miles to the east of Vitoria, they were put up in the house of the postmaster, his wife, and his daughter-in-law. Audícana, though now unimportant, was at that time the main village in the district of Barundia. Hence the post house. It lies on one of the main roads from France to Santiago de Compostela, and on the river Zadorra, which flows on to Vitoria. In the distance one can see the highest mountain of the Basque country, Monte Gorbea, a point of reference for miles around. Not far away to the north was the Cistercian monastery of Barria. The church of the village is large. It is characterised by a row of stone seats outside, on which presumably the good people of Audícana would in the eighteenth century have sat waiting for the service to begin. That suggests that the place was bigger in Beaumarchais's time than now. Audícana then even had a prison. Presumably the post house was on the main road below the church near a mediaeval bridge. There are still a number of large old houses which look as if they could once have served in that capacity.

As to those who lived there: "Ah, what a daughter-in-law," Beaumarchais wrote to the banker Durand about the postmaster and his family.

> Venus has never seen her like with such a face and such a figure. The most cruel of my adventures was to drink the very vanillaed cocoa which the Duque de San Blas had given me, together with some fresh eggs, the combination of which so warmed my blood that my ears are swollen as well as my nose, all my body is on fire, I have the devil's own headache, piles, exhaustion. . . . I had continuously to go to the water closet. . . . You would never guess what

followed. I had been given a great bar of health-giving chocolate. Imagine the combination of cacao and vanilla which I took.

All the students of the place where I had dinner with this beautiful daughter-in-law . . . were waiting for her, wanting to pay her court. They sang seguidillas with the guitar and then, even though I was tired, I was obliged to dance a minuet *alla françese,* which means that you take the left hand of your partner, raise it above your head, twirl her round twice, then stop her by slipping your arm around her back and then incline your head to hers. I begged the girl to perform this with me, even though these honest people had never seen such a thing. What cruelty, the beauty did not get up till ten o'clock and Vidal [the coachman] made me leave at six. . . . Give, my dear Durand, this news to Madame de Croix promptly . . . and tell my sisters.

The mystery about this recollection is where the students could have come from. Perhaps they were being educated in the nearby Cistercian monastery.

On his way home to Paris, Beaumarchais stopped at Orléans and called on the bishop, Monseigneur de Jarente, uncle of Madame de Croix, and gave him two boxes of cacao, which had been sent him by her. A few days later, he dined with the bishop in Paris. Beaumarchais reported to Durand that the bishop's attachment to his relations in Madrid was as sincere as it was lively. His mistress, Mademoiselle de Jarente, the marquesa's sister, seemed to Beaumarchais "strange and vivacious," and she said and did many things to please the taste of the indulgent prelate, whose character, he thought, was as sweet as his heart was excellent and his spirit enlightened.

Beaumarchais must have found Paris somewhat altered, for Madame de Pompadour had died during his absence. Yet the "douceur de vivre," the elegance of life, would last there nearly another twenty-five years and more.

Beaumarchais, despite his undoubted social triumphs (largely obtained by lavish spending of Pâris-Duverney's money), had not really enjoyed a successful visit to Madrid. He had, it is true, outwitted José Clavijo, but he had not arranged for his sister's marriage to him, and it turned out that that clever author would soon recover the royal favour. Beaumarchais had failed to secure for France the monopoly for the slave trade to the Spanish empire. The monopoly of provisioning of the Spanish army had also eluded him, as had the scheme for colonists in the Sierra Morena. The control of trade in Louisiana remained in Spanish hands, and the debtors of his father did not all pay their old bills. His clever idea of putting Madame de Croix in the bed of the king as a French agent had failed. But he returned to Paris with something more valuable: a myth of Spain which survives today, a treasury of interesting memories, of ingenious men and women of all classes which he put to good use in his plays, *The Barber of Seville*, *The Marriage of Figaro*, and the much less famous *The Guilty Mother.* Of course all writers invent characters. But what Beaumarchais found in Spain was a wonderfully lively society, and a way of life which allowed his characters to flourish.

These characters were, first and foremost, the Count of Almaviva, whom Beaumarchais causes to be *corregidor* of Andalusia in *The Barber of Seville.* The name of this nobleman probably derives from Madame de Croix's sometime lover Monseigneur Acquaviva, papal vice legate in Avignon. Almaviva's property, "three leagues outside Seville," in *The Marriage of Figaro,* was called Aguas Frescas, clear waters, which may seem to echo the title of the Marqués de Aguas Claras, who owned a fine palace in Havana next to the cathedral. But that title was not created till 1833. Aguas Frescas might perhaps have been an olive farm on the way to Huelva. But it was a real "castle in Spain."

As to the office which Beaumarchais gives the count, there were never any corregidors of large territories such as Andalusia, so that title of Almaviva's was a designation of fantasy. A corregidor was the Crown's representative on a city council. He was an official who expressed the spirit of the royal aspiration to central control in a city such as Seville (though the corregidor of Seville was actually known as the *asistente*).

In *The Marriage of Figaro,* we learn that Almaviva intended to accept the offer of the Spanish embassy in London. What a pity we do not know of his stay in London! "Ah, God damn it," as Figaro would have said. For he insists, in *The Marriage of Figaro,* act III, scene 3, that the use of those words was all that one needed in England to get anything done. Perhaps Almaviva would have fathered as many illegitimate children in London as one predecessor, the Duke of Feria, is supposed to have done in the embassy in the sixteenth century.

We learn from *The Guilty Mother* that Almaviva later became viceroy of Mexico. That great place had been filled by the husbands of Beaumarchais's two closest women friends in Madrid, the Conde de Fuenclara and the Marqués de Croix. In *The Guilty Mother*, however, Almaviva is living in Paris to enable him to sell his Spanish assets so as to leave his fortune to his "ward," Florestine, and disinherit his son León, whom he suspects, rightly, of being illegitimate. He seems, for tactical reasons, to have become a Republican, since he insists on being called "Monsieur" Almaviva, while the countess goes around Paris without a footman. France had become, after all, as Almaviva's disloyal secretary, Major Bégearss, says, "a headstrong country," which permitted divorce (*Mother*, act III, scene 9).

As for Almaviva's personality, his theory of life was summed up in the declaration "After three years, marriage becomes so respectable" (*Marriage*, act V, scene 7), and, as Figaro says in respect of him (*Mother*, act IV, scene 18), "Anger, in good hearts, represents only a pressing need to forgive." It has been fancifully suggested that the Duc de Choiseul, the French foreign minister who gave Beaumarchais his letters to the Spanish ministers Grimaldi and Squillace, was the origin of this famous figure.

Perhaps in some ways Beaumarchais modelled Almaviva on

the Marqués de Croix. Croix, after all, had several appointments similar to those of Almaviva: he was governor-general of Galicia, if not corregidor of Andalusia. He was not an ambassador, but he did become in 1766 viceroy in Mexico, as does the fictional Almaviva. He must, too, have gone to considerable trouble to marry such a beautiful girl as Madame de Croix was in 1764.

Rosine, the countess, is said in *The Barber of Seville* (act I, scene 4) to be of noble blood. One English translator of this play could not resist adding that she was a duke's daughter, a distinction which Beaumarchais did not give her. Figaro says (act I, scene 2) that she is "the prettiest girl, sweet, tender, affable, fresh, stimulating to the appetite, with a stealthy tread, good figure, graceful, plump bottom, red mouth, and what cheeks, what teeth, what hands!" She and the count had one son who was killed in a duel about 1788. While the count was away as viceroy in Mexico, she remained in Spain, just as the Condesa de Fuenclara and Madame de Croix had done when their husbands held the same office. Rosine goes to live in Astorga, a poor region in northwest Castile, on a rundown estate which Almaviva had bought from Cherubin's parents. There she has an affair with, and a son by, Cherubin. This was the Chevalier Léon, who plays an important part in *The Guilty Mother*.

The name Rosine may have an ancestry. For Rosalia was the name of the heroine of Diderot's *Fils naturel,* a play which Beaumarchais liked, and he had, before 1764, a close friend, Pauline le Breton. Perhaps "Rosine" was a mixture of "Rosalia" and "Pauline."

It is not easy to see on whom Rosine was based unless it was Beaumarchais's sister Lisette, who certainly seems to have suffered from the ups and downs of fortune. But perhaps she was unhappier than Rosine, since she never married and had no children that we know of. The Marquesa de Croix seemed much more in control of her affairs than was Rosine. She is not a strong candidate to be the original of Rosine.

Figaro, the immortal barber, is to Beaumarchais what Don Quixote is to Cervantes, Hamlet to Shakespeare. As has been suggested, he derives something of his capable personality from the central character of Ramón de la Cruz's sainete "El Barbero," which was shown for the first time while Beaumarchais was in Madrid. That play gives the barber control of events, even though he is in love—with a certain Manuela, who does not appear. Figaro's name perhaps comes from a taurine term *un figaro torera*, meaning a tight jacket used by bullfighters. Others insist that it signifies Fi-Caron, or *fils de Caron*, son of Caron. Or was it an anagram of For[t] gai? Beaumarchais spelled the character's name Figuaro in his first draft.

Often in those days barbers were barber-surgeons, qualified to bleed their clients as well as cut their hair, and that is what the barber does in Ramón de la Cruz's work. But Figaro had had aspirations to be more than a barber. In *The Barber of Seville*, Figaro is an ex-employee (valet?) of Almaviva whom the count had recommended in Madrid to a minister for employment and who is also portrayed as a would-be writer. He relates (in *Marriage*, act V, scene 3) that he has cobbled together a comedy in verse about the customs of the harem, assuming that "as a Spanish writer I can say what I like about Muhammad without drawing hostile fire. Next, some envoy from God knows where complains that, in my play, I have offended the Sublime Porte, Persia, a large slice of the Indian peninsula, the whole of Egypt, and the kingdoms of Barca, Tripoli, Tunisia, Algeria, and Morocco. And so my comedy dies all to placate Muslim princes, not one of whom so far as I know can read but who beat us black and blue and say we are Christian dogs." These reflections, it will be observed, have a twenty-first-century character.

In *The Marriage of Figaro,* Figaro is again valet to the count but also concierge of his château at Aguas Frescas. He is the hero of *The Guilty Mother,* and, at the end of that play, saves the count from catastrophe.

Figaro's philosophy is summed up in his song at the end of *The Marriage of Figaro* (act V, scene 19):

> *By the luck of birth,*
> *Nature makes us king or shepherd,*
> *Chance makes the distance*
> *Only wit can make a difference.*
> *Out of twenty kings who wear a crown*
> *Death breaks the altar,*
> *But Voltaire is immortal.*

The last phrase recalls the astonishing place which Voltaire had in French life at the time of the production of *The Barber of Seville.*

Figaro's attitude towards his master is irreverent but affectionate. In *The Barber of Seville* (act V, scene 12) he tells the count: "You command everything here except yourself." At the end of *The Guilty Mother,* Figaro seems to have become a French revolutionary; when opposing the idea of duels, he says that from now on "one will fight only the enemies of the state" (act V, scene 7; a sentence which two English translators enthusiastically render: "the enemies of France").

Barbers were familiar figures in Beaumarchais's time, for few Spaniards shaved themselves. Anyone of any pretence to rank, too, would have the barber visit him, instead of him visiting the barber. The barber's visit would often coincide with visits by the client's friends. "How erudite he might have been had he spent as much time on study as he did on his coiffure," says a character in another of Ramón de la Cruz's plays. Hairdressers were always going to the houses of their female clients too, spending hours there, seeking to copy the high coiffures of the French, as well as applying all sorts of creams and pomades to their clients, whom they would also tease.

Figaro became famous for his radical views. He addresses the count (though not to his face): "You think that because you are a great lord, you are a genius. Nobility, wealth, rank, high position! Such things make people proud. But what did you ever do to earn them? You took the trouble to be born, that's all. For the rest, a very ordinary man" (*Marriage,* act V, scene 3). It is this speech, perhaps, that caused Danton to say that "Figaro killed off the nobility." Napoleon, rather mysteriously, said that *The Marriage of Figaro* was "the revolution in action"; he should have known, for Metternich would name him "the revolution incarnate."

In *The Barber of Seville*, Figaro tells Rosine that "only imbeciles get fat on boredom" (act II, scene 2). He also points out that one must have a status in society, a family, a name, a rank, influence, to make a sensation in the world while at the same time insulting it ("Il faut un état, une famille, un nom, un rang, de la constance enfin por faire sensation dans le monde en calomniant"; act II, scene 9). Voltaire might have said much the same. Figaro tells Bartholo, the second-rate lawyer of Seville, that he would have "his work cut out to find anyone cleverer than he" (*Barber*, act III, scene 10). But even Almaviva, when he is pretending to be a horse doctor, says things which would not normally be said in polite society: for example, he points out to Bartholo that medicine is an art tremendously beneficial—to those who practice it (act II, scene 13).

Such bold declarations mark the works of Beaumarchais at every point. Even the usually docile and innocent Rosine thinks it intolerable that anyone should think that he has the right to open somebody else's letters (act II, scene 15). "What gives you the right?" she demands of Bartholo. "The oldest right in the world. The right of the strong," he replies (act II, scene 15). In *The Marriage of Figaro* the countess says that Figaro exudes such confidence that some of it was wearing off on her (act II, scene 3). He at one point in the same play tells his master that he knows that "he gives her presents but he is unfaithful" (act III, scene 5). Once when the count suggests that, with his originality and intelligence, Figaro might go far, he replies: "Promoted? For intelligence? You're laughing at me, sir. If you're mediocre and prepared to crawl, I agree you can go anywhere" (act V, scene 5). He also insists that tribunals are "indulgent to the rich, tough on the weak." In *The Guilty Mother*, he says to the count that to allow Bégearss to retain, out of pique, the inheritance that he immorally extracted is to be not virtuous but feeble: "What do you get from loyalty if perfidy is paid so well?"

Suzanne in *The Marriage of Figaro*, maid to the countess, wants to marry Figaro and eventually does so, avoiding the attentions of Almaviva with some difficulty. The count boasts that he has just abandoned the right of sleeping with all the prospective brides on his estate—but that alleged right had in truth not existed in Andalusia for many generations, if it ever formally did. Suzanne, too, has sometimes a scathing attitude towards the upper classes. Thus in *The Marriage of Figaro* she says: "I have seen how the customs of high society enable ladies to be able to lie without seeming to" (act II, scene 24). But in *The Guilty Mother* she too becomes conventional: thus she does not approve of Almaviva in Paris calling himself "Monsieur" because it reflects on her own and Figaro's status.

The pert exchanges of Suzanne and Figaro with their master echo many comparable conversations in sainetes. In "El Hablador" (The talker, of Ramón de la Cruz), when a guest speaks of having walked from one end of Madrid to the other, a maid answers: "Well, I've walked more. . . . I've walked from the bed to the kitchen, from the kitchen to the mirror, from the mirror to the stove, from the stove to the sink, from the sink to the chopping block, from the chopping block to the dish shelf, from the dish shelf to the pot shelf." In "El Trueque de las Criadas" (The barter of the servants), another such play, we hear the master ask, "What time is it?" A servant answers: "I don't know because the clock in the square and mine too have stopped." "Why do you talk like that to your master? . . . I am fed up with you." "Well, sir, eat a little rhubarb. That always helps people who are fed up." "If your tongue could stop wagging." "And yours too."

These insolent opinions have usually been supposed to be those of Beaumarchais himself, and he relished that reputation. Napoleon's comment about his role in the revolution would have delighted him, had he heard it. But Beaumarchais was, like many writers, an ambiguous personality. His poetic criticism of the slave trade was, we have seen, followed by his pursuit of the monopoly of taking slaves into the Spanish empire in collaboration with his commercial mentor, Pâris-Duverney. Then in 1775 his hostility to the slave trade once more came to the fore. When young he had evidently wanted to be a nobleman at the same time as presenting himself as the incorrigible Jean-Bête. He delighted in his success at court: he loved and profited from his friendship with the princesses to whom he taught music. True, he came from a relatively humble background, and his father had chosen to convert to Catholicism in order to exercise his profession as a watchmaker in Paris. He was certainly sometimes snubbed in his early days at Versailles. But despite some disdainful comments by aristocrats of ancient lineage, such as the Duc de la Rochefoucauld, Beaumarchais's self-confidence and cheek carried him through to royal favour as well as to prosperity.

Figaro was a brilliant character, much more radical in the plays than he turns out to be in the operas of Mozart and Rossini. Afterwards Beaumarchais did not object at all to adapting himself to his own creation. But if the ancien régime had renewed itself rather than destroyed itself in 1789, Beaumarchais would have found a way to come out on the winning side, laughing. He was nothing if not a survivor. Figaro's radicalism reflected the mood of imaginative and inventive servants; but his creator was not his exemplar.

Marceline is the housekeeper in the count's castle of Aguas Frescas. She turns out to be the mother of Figaro by Bartholo, whom she marries at the end of the play. She makes a good feminist speech in *The Marriage of Figaro* (act IV, scene 16): "We, poor oppressed women, are more than prepared to defend ourselves against the whole of the proud, terrible, and really rather simple-minded male sex."

Antonio, the gardener at Aguas Frescas, the uncle of Suzanne, also has radical moments. Thus in *The Marriage of Figaro* (act II, scene 21) he says, half-drunk, to Almaviva: "If you haven't enough up there," pointing to his head, "to keep hold of a good servant, I am not so stupid as to let go of a good master such as you are."

Cherubin, one of the most original figures in these plays, after Figaro, is page to the count in *The Marriage of Figaro*. In Cherubin, Beaumarchais must surely have been thinking of himself in his own childhood, surrounded by so many women in his father's house in the rue Saint-Denis. But the amorous pageboy is a commonplace of the Renaissance. Shakespeare makes fun of the idea in *Twelfth Night*. *The Guilty Mother* reveals that his real name is León de Astorga. He is distantly related to Rosine and is also her godson (*Marriage*, act I, scene 10). He loves women indiscriminately: in *The Marriage of Figaro* he says, "These last few days, I've felt my heart pound every time I see a woman. The words 'love' and 'tender' make it race" (act I, scene 7). Yet he becomes a soldier. In *The Guilty Mother* it becomes clear that he had an affair in the province of Astorga with the countess (while the count was in Mexico) and had a son, León, by her. When he learns that Rosine is pregnant by himself, in remorse he takes part in a frontal attack on a fort and is killed. His blood-stained letter to her is in the jewel case which Almaviva opens theatrically in *The Guilty Mother* (act II, scene 1).

Pages in sainetes usually cut a pitiful figure. Cursed was the page "who has not seven pairs of legs, one for every day of the week." The page had to deliver all invitations to his mistress's tertulias, buy candles, hire musicians, deliver letters of condolence and congratulation, take round Christmas presents, reserve seats at the theatre, pay bills, or escort guests up or down, as well as accompany his mistress wherever she wanted, usually walking behind her coach.

The one character in Beaumarchais's plays who seems to have no radical views is Bartholo, a doctor of Seville and guardian of Rosine, whom he hopes to marry, in *The Barber of Seville*. He turns out to be the father of Figaro, and in the end he marries Marceline, Figaro's mother, at the end of the play, a Wildean touch more than

Marin, from whose intolerance Beaumarchais later suffered in Paris. He does not like being told what to do. He says on one occasion, "I haven't come to the castle to carry out commissions" (*Marriage*, act II, scene 22).

Other characters are international. The Chevalier Léon is the son of the Countess Almaviva by Cherubino, according to *The Guilty Mother*. Living in Paris, he seems to have become very French in his loyalties: his future, he thinks, is simple: "Under the simple uniform of a soldier, I will defend the liberty of our new fatherland. An unknown man, I will either die for her or serve her as a zealous citizen" (act IV, scene 18). Then the villain of *The Guilty Mother* is Major Honoré Bégearss, an Irishman, a former secretary of the count when ambassador in London. Bégearss had been a major in the cavalry. His job had been to encode official papers and, in the process, like other secretaries, he managed to get hold of family secrets. His philosophy is that "politics calls for superior talents and is threatened by one thing only: honest principles" (*Mother*, act IV, scene 4). He is outwitted by Figaro in the nick of time. Though he puts himself forward as the right man to marry Florestine, Almaviva's ward and illegitimate daughter, Figaro finds that in Ireland he has a wife already. His name is mysterious: "Bécasse" (woodcock) was the nickname of Beaumarchais's favourite sister, Julie. But it can also mean idiot.

All these persons, so well-known to the theatrical and opera-going public, could have appeared in a sainete of Ramón de la Cruz, and some did. Yet all their characters were deepened by

Beaumarchais. Figaro's commentaries on the social structure are not just pert, they are profound as well as witty. The Count of Almaviva is much cleverer, say, than "el señor del Pueblo" in Ramón de la Cruz's "Las Frioleras" (The baubles). The sainetes were obviously written in Spanish. But though most of Beaumarchais's creations have Spanish names and nationalities, and live in or near Seville, they are men and women with international and timeless identities.

Postscript

The future of Beaumarchais and his friends varied considerably. He himself, through his plays, attained glory. His first play after arriving back in Paris was *Eugénie,* performed in 1767, a work set in an imaginary London, whose mythical qualities he did not capture as well as he would Seville. But he did invent a valet de chambre of the debauched "Comte de Clarendon" whose name was, appropriately for eighteenth-century London, Drink. Then, in imitation of what he had seen in Madrid, he wrote what appears to be a sainete, "The Sacristan." We can see in this work, never completed, and for two hundred years unknown, the first appearance of Bartholo, a Lindor who anticipates the Count of Almaviva, and an engaging Pauline/Rosina; but there is no Figaro. There followed *Les Deux Amis,* a play set among businessmen of Lyon, which was first performed in January 1770. It was a failure.

The Barber of Seville was first performed, with the subtitle *The Useless Precaution,* in February 1775, *The Marriage of Figaro* in 1784. Its subtitle was *The Mad Day. The Guilty Mother,* the third, much less popular play in the series, was performed in 1790. The first two plays made Beaumarchais famous. Mozart's opera *The Marriage of Figaro,* based on Beaumarchais's work, was first presented in 1786, and Rossini's *The Barber of Seville,* similarly based, in 1816. The reason why Mozart did not himself make use of *The Barber of Seville* was probably because the productive Neapolitan Giovanni Paesiello had already had a great success in St. Petersburg with his own opera based on that play. Mozart and Leopoldo da Ponte persuaded the enlightened Emperor Leopold that they could present the plot as a comedy, not as the dramatic justification for social revolution which it had seemed in France. Since then, rare has been the year when productions of the operas have not been somewhere performed. Beaumarchais's characters are thus always with us, though those who admire the operas do not always know whose was the invention which they applaud.

Meanwhile, Beaumarchais published a brief memoir about his dealings with Clavijo. It so impressed the twenty-five-year-old Goethe in Germany that he based his first play on it. The work, which is still sometimes performed, ends with the death of Lisette and a duel in which Clavijo is killed. Beaumarchais himself saw it in Augsburg in 1774, though he seems to have made no comment.

Beaumarchais found on his return to Paris that his friend Pierre Lartigues of Nantes had ascertained that Pauline le Breton's property in Saint-Domingue, in the quartier Dulimbet, was beautiful and in good productive land. It had been neglected, but eighteen months of hard work could make it again into a fine sugar plantation, which would bring in 180,000 livres a year. The family of Mademoiselle le Breton was highly respectable, he learned.

But the news was no longer useful to him since Pauline, in Beaumarchais's absence, had become enamoured of her cousin, the Chevalier de Seguirand, and would soon marry him. Early in June 1764 Beaumarchais had written to Pauline: "Listen, my pretty child, the law of the pen must be the motor of our sentiments. Anyone who reflects before writing to his mistress is a deceitful swindler. And what does it matter if a letter is well written or that the periods are balanced?" Perhaps from this Pauline had concluded that this brilliant admirer who was also an adventurer might not be an ideal husband?

But Beaumarchais did marry, twice more, and have children, and his descendants proudly flourish. His extraordinarily complicated financial and political life has been amply chronicled, above all by Maurice Lever, and does not need to figure in this essay. Here one should note that the weapons which Beaumarchais arranged for delivery to the United States may have been decisive in winning the battle of Saratoga for the rebels. Beaumarchais once aspired to be French consul in Madrid, but Choiseul took against him because he appeared to have exceeded his powers in his activities in Spain.

Pâris-Duverney died in 1770, and the disputes over his will and old debts engulfed his family and Beaumarchais.

As for Beaumarchais's friends and acquaintances in Spain, Clavijo lived on till 1806, when he died aged seventy-six. He was restored to a degree of royal favour soon after Beaumarchais left Madrid. He never married, either scared away from the idea by his astonishing experiences with Beaumarchais or because something within him, which should have been evident in the 1760s, made him a man who did not wish to marry: perhaps that explained his conduct with Lisette.

He became famous as a naturalist and was secretary of the Royal Society of Natural History from its foundation. Then in 1770 he became director of the Theatre of the Court. He wrote several books, translated part of Buffon's *Histoire Naturelle, Générale et Particulière* into Spanish and, from 1773 to 1799, was the editor of *El Mercurio Histórico y Político de Madrid,* a monthly journal. At first this was a copy of the *Mercure de la Haye,* but in 1784 it became a worthwhile Spanish production of its own, even if the news which it included had almost always been published before by its rival, the older semiweekly, *Gaceta,* an official paper of the government. Clavijo had difficulties with the Inquisition in 1780 but otherwise he seems to have lived calmly.

Grimaldi remained minister for foreign affairs till 1776 and died ten years later. Richard Wall, Clavijo's benefactor before 1764, and Beaumarchais's, briefly, died shortly after he returned from Aranjuez to Granada. Buturlin died in office as ambassador in 1767 and

María returned to Russia post haste. The king of Spain lived on till 1788, enacting many useful reforms; on his deathbed, he is supposed to have told the prior of the monastery of El Escorial, "Father, I never had any other woman than she whom God gave me."

As for Beaumarchais's other connections in Madrid, the Marqués de Croix was named viceroy of Mexico in 1766. He arrived at his new post with an entourage of thirty, including many Frenchmen. He became renowned as an enlightened but autocratic proconsul who introduced important reforms in the administration of New Spain. He also took the remarkable step of expelling the Jesuits from Mexico, following the decisions of the government at home. Trade was also freed. These reforms led to the invention of a new Mexico, which embarked on the adventure of independence in the 1820s.

On Croix's return to Spain, he became captain-general of Valencia, where he died in 1786 aged eighty-three.

His beautiful wife did not accompany him to Mexico nor to Valencia, but, after Beaumarchais, she seems to have had no more intrigues, and gave herself up to religion. The Baron de Gleichen in Paris remembers her as retaining her wonderful looks into old age. "She exists only for the poor," wrote Baron Gleichen, who added that she also remained vivacious to the end of her life. Her lover in Avignon before she met Beaumarchais, Monseigneur Acquaviva, became a cardinal in 1770.

Beaumarchais's travelling companion on the way to Madrid, the Marquis d'Aubarède, returned to France after numerous adventures.

Playing his cards well at the risk of his life, in his seventies he was made a maréchal de camp by the Revolution and then, in 1793, military councillor to the committee for public health.

Changes were already afoot in Madrid by the time Beaumarchais left. From 1765 a director and a large staff were appointed to give lighting to the city during the winter from nightfall to midnight. Householders were obliged to sweep their entrances daily and put their rubbish in special boxes. Dogs without identification could henceforth be shot. It is true that the Marqués de Squillace failed to secure the prohibition of the wearing of long cloaks as part of his battle against crime; but a similar measure was later carried through by the Conde de Aranda. Enlightened government followed. The famous night watchmen, the *serenos,* were to be seen in Madrid before the end of the 1760s, and their presence much restricted crime at night.

In this seemingly new city the sisters of Beaumarchais continued their lives in the Calle de la Montera. Lisette did not marry —not even Jean Durand. The Beaumarchais family in Paris seems not to have maintained further close relations with the two sisters. The Condesa de Fuenclara lived on in her splendid house in the Calle de Hortaleza till 1785, when she died aged eighty-six. Beaumarchais's real friends in Madrid, his creations, live on, ever youthful, to this day.

Bibliography

SOURCES

The main sources for this book are the writings of Beaumarchais contained in his plays and memoirs, best seen in the Pléiade edition of his works, the first volume of his letters edited by Brian Morton, and his *Memoire d'Espagne,* published long ago by Édouard Fournier. The two chapters on Spain in the late Maurice Lever's admirable life of Beaumarchais were most useful as a beginning. What a tragedy he died just after completing his third volume! I greatly benefited from rereading the *sainetes* of Ramón de la Cruz and a brilliant forgotten book about Madrid in the eighteenth century by the late Charles Kany. For Clavijo, I read Jean Sarrailh's magnificent study of the enlightenment in Spain. All these works are listed below. I was fortunate enough to have had the pleasure of discussing Beaumarchais with his generous descendant, Jean-Pierre de Beaumarchais, who has shown me some important material in his family archives.

Principal Works Consulted

Arnould, E. J. *La genèse du Barbier de Seville.* Dublin: CNRS, 1962.

Baillie, G. H. *Watches.* London, 1929.

Beaumarchais, Jean-Pierre de, ed., *Beaumarchais l'écrivain de la liberté.* Paris: Les éditions de la bouteille á la Mer, 1999.

Beaumarchais, Pierre-Augustin Caron de. *Correspondance.* 4 vols. Ed. Brian Morton. Paris: Nizet, 1969–1987.

———. *Oeuvres.* Ed. Pierre Larthomas. Paris: Gallimard [Bibliothèque de la Pléiade], 1988.

———. *Oeuvres complètes de Beaumarchais.* Ed. Edouard Fournier. Paris: Laplace, Sánchez, 1876. (This includes the *Memoire sur l'Espagne,* written as a letter to the Duke of Choiseul, 1765. It is the basis for Chapter 7.)

Besterman, Theodore. *Voltaire.* London: Longmans, 1969.

Bourgoing, J.-F. de. *Travels in Spain.* Dublin: P. Byrne and W. Jones, 1790.

Burckhardt, Jacob. *The Civilisation of the Renaissance in Italy.* London: Phaidon, 1950.

Calderón Quijana, J. A. *Los Virreyes de Nueva España en el Reino de Carlos III.* 2 vols. Seville: Escuela de Estudios Hispano-Americanos de Sevilla, 1967.

Carlos III y La Ilustración. 2 vols. Madrid: Ministerio de Cultura, 1988.

Casanova, Giacomo. *Histoire de ma vie.* 12 vols. Wiesbaden, 1960–1962.

Cruz, Ramón de la. *Sainetes.* Ed. Emilio Costarelo. Madrid: Nueva Biblioteca de Autores Españoles, vols. 23 (1915), 26 (1928). ("El Barbero" can be found in vol. 23, 131–137.)

Donvez, Jacques. "La politique de Beaumarchais." BN microfiche 15679. (This consists of a transcription of seven volumes of manuscript archives in the Comédie Française.)

Ezquerra del Bayo, Joaquín. *Catálogo General Ilustrado: El Abanico en España.* Madrid: Sociedad Española de los Amigos del Arte, 1920.

Fernán-Núñez, Conde de. *Vida de Carlos III.* Madrid: Librería de Fernando Fé, 1898.

Franklin, Alfred. *La vie privée d'autrefois, la vie de Paris sous Louis XV.* Paris, 1899.

Gleichen, Baron Charles-Henri. *Souvenirs.* Ed. Paul Grimblot. Paris: Léon Techener fils, 1868.

Goethe, Johann Wolfgang. *Clavigo: Ein Trauerspiel.* Leipzig, 1774.

Gómez Aparicio, Pedro. *Historia del periodismo español.* 2 vols. Madrid: Editora Nacional, 1967.

Goncourt, Edmond and Jules. *Madame de Pompadour.* Paris: Firmin Didot, 1888.

Gudin de la Brenellerie, Paul-Philippe. *Histoire de Beaumarchais.* Ed. M. Tourneaux. Paris: Plon, 1888.

Hemingway, Ernest. *Death in the Afternoon.* London: Jonathan Cape, 1932.

Herr, Richard. *The Eighteenth-Century Revolution in Spain.* Princeton: Princeton University Press, 1958.

Jovellanos, Gaspar Melchor de. *Obras Completas.* 7 vols. Ed. José Miguel Caso. Oviedo: Centro de Estudios del Siglo XVIII, 1984.

Kany, Charles E. *Life and Manners in Madrid, 1750–1800.* Berkeley: University of California Press, 1932.

Labat, Jean-Baptiste. *Voyages aux isles,* ed. Michel Le Bris. Paris: Phébus, 1993.

Langle, Marquis de. *Voyage de Figaro en Espagne.* Saint-Malo, 1784.

Larthomas, Pierre. *Parades.* Paris: SEDES, 1977.

Lever, Maurice. *Pierre-Augustin Caron de Beaumarchais.* 2 vols. Paris: Fayard, 1999–2003.

Llorente, J. A. *Historia Crítica de la Inquisición.* 2 vols. Barcelona: J. Pons, 1870–1880.

Loménie, Louis de. *Beaumarchais et son temps.* 2 vols. Paris: Michel-Lévy, 1856.

Madariaga, Isabel de. *Russia in the Age of Catherine the Great.* London: Weidenfeld and Nicolson, 1981.

Madrid Villa y Corte. 3 vols. Madrid: Silex, 1987.

Olavide, Pablo de. *Obras Selectas.* Lima: Banco de Crédito del Perú, 1987.

Petrie, Sir Charles, Bt. *King Charles III of Spain.* London: Constable, 1971.

Pomeau, René. *Beaumarchais ou la bizarre destinée.* Paris: PUF, 1987.

Proschwitz, Gunnar von. *Beaumarchais and "The Courier of Europe."* Oxford: Studies on Voltaire at the Taylor Institution, 1990.

Proust, Jacques. "Précisions nouvelles sur les débuts de Pierre-Augustin Caron de Beaumarchais." *Studi Francesi,* January–April 1963, 85–88.

Sarrablo Aguareles, Eugenio. *El Conde de Fuenclara, Embajador y Virrey de Nueva España.* 2 vols. Seville: Escuela de Estudios Hispano-Americanos de Sevilla, 1955–1966.

Sarrailh, Jean. *Espagne éclairée de la seconde moitié du XVIII siècle.* Paris: Librairie C. Klincksieck, 1964.

Seebacher, J. "Autour de Figaro: Beaumarchais, la famille de Choiseul et le financier Clavière." *Revue de l'Histoire littéraire de la France* 62 (1962), 198–228.

Sorel, Albert. *Europe and the French Revolution: The Political Traditions of the Old Régime.* Trans. and ed. Alfred Cobban and J. W. Hunt. London: Collins, 1969.

Stein, Stanley, and Barbara H. Stein. *Apogee of Empire.* Baltimore: Johns Hopkins University Press, 2003.

Tapia, Enrique de. *Carlos III y su época.* Madrid: Aguilar, 1963.

Torres y Ramírez, Bibiano. *La Compañía Gaditana de Negros.* Seville: Escuela de Estudios Hispano-Americanos, 1973.

Townsend, Joseph. *Journey through Spain in 1786–87.* London: C. Dilly, 1792.

Index